W9-DHR-732

Praise for the Second Book in the Series:
Ministry in a Church Dismantled—To Tear Down or Build Up?

Many of us Christians have wondered where God is during this pandemic. It's hard to see the hand of God in all the confusion, conflict, suffering, and death. Sociologist and pastor Conrad Kanagy has a provocative proposal: God is using the pandemic (among other things) to dismantle the church. This is a disruptive book. But like Isaiah's vision for the people of God in exile, Kanagy also imagines comfort and healing in a new kind of church where every member is a minister and a missionary, where complex questions about racism, sexism, and socialism are welcomed, and where Jesus rather than politics is at the center of the community of faith. He references the self-governing, self-financing, and self-propagating philosophy of 19th-century missionaries in India (which in one of those curious twists of history has become the official philosophy of the Three-Self Protestant Church in China) and sees a church called into the world where we find Jesus already present among the poor, marginalized and oppressed. Kanagy ends the book in a dark tunnel. Is the light at the end of the tunnel an approaching train? Or is the distant light a reflection of the face of Jesus? In the darkness of the tunnel, we sometimes stumble in doubt and uncertainty. But Kanagy assures us that the hope drawing us toward the light of Christ will not disappoint. "We shall see him face to face."

- Nate Showalter, International Pastor

Praise for the First Book in the Series: *A Church Dismantled—
A Kingdom Restored: Why Is God Taking Apart the Church?*

———————————

I found this book to be compelling. Kanagy's numerous thought-provoking questions challenged me to ask myself these questions. Am I allowing the Holy Spirit to move in my life and in my church instead of giving way to my need to control and predict? Can I believe God's truth that he loves His Church and me with a perfect love – even with our imperfections? Do I believe that God is active, engaged, and omnipresent in our communities and our world during the isolation and loneliness of the pandemic? What am I learning during this pandemic? Kanagy pointed out that Covid-19 may ultimately be a gift to the church! Can I cultivate a spirit of gratitude rather than bemoaning what has been lost? Can I host a neighborhood party instead of ranting on Facebook? The Parkinson's Disease diagnosis has enabled Kanagy to share deeply about his personal "dismantling" and to compare that to the church. Can I trust that God is up to something good in my life and the life of the Church? Yes, Kanagy raised many salient questions to ponder, pray about, discuss, and answer. I want to be involved in the Church that God is restoring.

- Julia Sensenig, College Professor

If it is for freedom that Christ has set us free (Galatians 5:1 NIV), then why is Conrad Kanagy, after a lifetime of following Christ and preaching the gospel, finally being set free? His journey with Parkinson's Disease led to an epiphany that converged with the Covid-19 pandemic. About this time, I began listening to his podcast (A Church Dismantled—A Kingdom Restored). Everything inside me that wanted to return to normalcy in my life (and the life of the church I pastor) was "checkmated." I thought about Gamaliel's wise words in Acts 5:38 that "if this plan or this undertaking is of human origin, it will fail; but if it is of God, you will not be able to overthrow them—in that case, you may even be found fighting against God!" If, as Kanagy suggests, we live in a liminal time or "crossing-over" space, then I ignore it at my own peril. So, what to do? I kept listening and reading, eager to hear more about what he was sensing and hearing with his Spirit-magnified vision. I was not surprised by how accurate his analysis was of the problems (especially among North American Evangelicals). The idea that the Spirit of God might be dismantling the church of Jesus Christ was not a new one. He has written on it in the past. What was new was Conrad's willingness to share with greater transparency and risky vulnerability, about how he, as a long-time Jesus follower, could see with increasing clarity the disparity between the Kingdom that Jesus proclaimed and the church that claims to follow him. For those of us in the church who have bartered away the radical truth of the gospel, he challenges us to spot the ways we have become captives to our culture (both secular and Christian). For those who have withdrawn from cultural engagement under the pretense of preserving purity, Conrad challenges us to give up our religious game-playing, get real and embrace the gospel of freedom (not fear). My favorite parts of the book are where Conrad tells himself the gospel truth in a way that is refreshingly hopeful (even in the face of the certainty of death). I will keep reading it repeatedly to wake myself up to the ways that I have fallen asleep in the light of Jesus Christ.

- Jim Laverty, Pastor

IN A CHURCH
DISMANTLED
THE LIGHT STILL SHINES

Reflections in
Sacred Time

CONRAD L. KANAGY

IN A CHURCH DISMANTLED
THE LIGHT STILL SHINES
Reflections in Sacred Time
by Conrad L. Kanagy

Copyright © 2021
All rights reserved.

Scripture quotations unless noted otherwise are from *The New Revised Standard Version of the Bible* (NRSV), copyright © 1989, Division of Christian Education of the National Council of the Churches of Christ in the United States of America. Used by permission. All rights reserved.

Library of Congress Control Number: 2021949236
International Standard Book Number: 978-1-60126-765-8

Masthof Press
219 Mill Road | Morgantown, PA 19543-9516
www.Masthof.com

MORE BY CONRAD L. KANAGY

A Church Dismantled—A Kingdom Restored: Why Is God Taking Apart the Church? Morgantown, PA: Masthof Press, 2021.

Ministry in a Church Dismantled: To Tear Down or Build Up? Morgantown, PA: Masthof Press, 2021.

Winds of the Spirit: A Profile of Anabaptist Churches in the Global South. (with Richard Showalter and Tilahun Beyene), Harrisonburg, VA: Herald Press, 2012.

Road Signs for the Journey: A Profile for Mennonite Church USA. Harrisonburg, VA: Herald Press, 2007.

The Riddles of Human Society (with Donald Kraybill), California: Pine Forge Press, 1999.

TO BOB BAKER

You have walked with me
through darkness and light.
In the end by Grace,
we are both finding our way home.

"The land be level and the water folded,
Trees gigantic and the walls built low."

—Reynolds Price, "All Will Be Whole" (after Rilke)

TABLE OF CONTENTS

PART ONE | 1
Finding My Way Through the Dark

PART TWO | 23
Out of the Darkness

FOREWORD

God is Light, and God expressed Light by speaking, "Let there be light." There is much light unseen in darkness to the natural eye—radio waves or ultraviolet, for example. However, the full range of electromagnetic energy extends well beyond the spectrum of light visible to the human eye. This is true in everyday life on the planet and in the spiritual realm.

In this very darkness, we meet the One who is Light. Herein, we may explore intriguing questions as to how God feels and sees our world. "He knows what is in the darkness, and light dwells with Him." (Daniel 2:22b NASB) In this darkness, the scriptures are the lamp to our feet and, therefore, a light to our path.

Because we are willing to look at the dismantledness of the church, we see ways God continues to creatively say, "Let there be light." That light exposes darkness for what it is, purports to be, but is not. In that illumination, we may consider our own motives and acknowledge where we have been, or are, in the dark.

Living in dismantledness is not for the faint of heart, but it is a setting for healthy questioning of what is, with a posture of reconstruction in mind. We gain additional perspective when we live with the day of our death in mind. While suffering, we find abundant hope in Christ, who suffered most severely all of the consequences of darkness.

Welcome to the community of Light Seekers who have engaged with Dr. Conrad Kanagy in podcasts and blogs. Sit with him in the college classroom, congregation, and sociology lab. Join him in devotional meditation, reminiscence of childhood, and reflection upon significant life experiences.

In the chapters that follow, you will see that you are deeply loved and not alone.

- Keith E. Yoder, Ed.D.
Founder, Teaching the Word Ministries

INTRODUCTION AND ACKNOWLEDGEMENTS

This volume is the third in the series entitled "A Church Dismantled—A Kingdom Restored," based on podcast episodes I wrote during the Covid-19 pandemic. These episodes, now chapters in the current book, were mainly written during Sacred Time of Advent, 2020, and Lent, 2021—usually in the midst of or immediately following my morning time with God and before I headed off to classes at Elizabethtown College. This is not a typical "devotional" book for either sacred season and might be just as beneficial to one's soul and "life with God" if read during Ordinary Time. On the other hand, with many themes related to Advent and Lent in the book, it will be significant if read during Sacred Time.

This book follows two previous and just published volumes, addressing themes related to God's dismantling of the church. This book does not so directly address the church's dismantling as do the other two, but instead seeks to identify the light that still shines in a dismantled church, a church that seems so much in the shadows and in the dark these days. But to understand the fuller context, I need to describe what I mean by the dismantling of the church.

For me, dismantling the Church is about joining God's grand excavation project of Isaiah 40 (which has captured my imagination ever since I was a child) by lowering mountains that are barriers to the shalom of God's coming kingdom, by raising valleys in which the marginalized have had to hide for fear of being overrun by those who hold the power strings, by making crooked paths straight and rough places a level plain along which the lost, the wounded, and the needy may find their way home.[1]

A second component to the dismantling of the church is the Spirit's removal of those "mantles" of our own devising that we have placed on the Church and the Christian faith. These cover up the truths of God's kingdom that we are called to live by as our truths. The dismantling I identify is also personal and autobiographical, as I confess my own false mantles while also calling out the false mantles of the Church—whether those false mantles be imposed upon any one or all of us, or upon God, or upon the Church itself.

From early on as a child, I was caught in cycles of torment and depression characteristic of obsessive-compulsiveness, which were fed by the oppressiveness of an "Old Order" cultural fog that emphasized goodness, performance, perfection, and, on top of it all, God's wrath. So whenever I failed to hit the high mark, which was every moment of every day, I remember having these kinds of thoughts: *Am I the only sinner among this bunch of saints? Are all the others okay with their sins? Do they know some secret about how to survive with a guilty conscience, which no one has shared with me? I don't understand why everyone says the gospel is so wonderful when it often feels like hell instead of good news.*

Slowly and over time, I began to understand that what the Church had done (and all too often still does) was to "mantle" (as in "muzzle") the truth by declaring one thing while being altogether comfortable at times with something else. To "mantle" means to cover up and smooth over. The Church has too often covered up truths

---

[1]   I will use lower-case church and upper-case Church interchangeably. While we can readily draw historical, theological and sociological distinctions between the two, such differentiation is beyond this book's intent. And such clear lines may only exist in our heads and textbooks.

and smoothed over falsehoods. It was recognizing the false mantles of the church for what they are that saved me from giving up on God. And I suspect that I will spend the rest of my days doing the work of dismantling if it means that even one more person could be set free, as I have been set free over this past year—set free by the One named Jesus who so dismantled the religious arrogance and towers of his day that it cost him his life to save the world.

In 2017, I was diagnosed with Parkinson's disease at the age of fifty-two. For the first year, I cried and raged as I grieved the losses to come. But over time, I have also begun to recognize the gifts that I am receiving due to this disease. One of those gifts is the clarity with which I now see the horizon ahead and the knowledge that my days of quality health are limited. This recognition has been transformative for me, as I realize that my own body is being dismantled at the same time that the Church itself is being dismantled. My weaknesses are being exposed; the mantles I wore to cover those weaknesses have been stripped away. I can't hide my vulnerabilities or deny my fragility. Over the past four years, I have had a new conversion to Jesus and a new awareness of God's incredible love for his children—meaning every human being is created with the imprint of God upon them. I have little doubt that the podcast or this book series would ever have emerged without this disease that took me by such surprise, but which I now realize is my own unique path home.

It has been clear to me during the past year that I am not alone in my sense that the Church is in the process of being dismantled. The podcast "A Church Dismantled—A Kingdom Restored" has appealed to many more listeners than I ever imagined it would. Nearly 50,000 episodes have been downloaded in more than eighty countries and almost 1,600 cities. It seems my writing has had a unique appeal to folks who have become disillusioned with the American Church and have perhaps left it. I call these folks "the diaspora"—

those who have left what we have long presumed to be the primary institution by which one discovers the kingdom of God but which too often is the one that leads folks in the wrong direction or in no direction at all.

I have many persons to acknowledge and thank for their support of this project over the past year and longer. I have walked with my wife Heidi for more than three decades through more darkness and light than with anyone else in the world. Some days it feels like we are both in the dark, and some days as if one of us is and the other is not. And then, on periodic days, it feels like we are both in the light together. Regardless, we have by the grace of God found our way through a more than two-year marriage separation, multiple bouts of cancer, numerous church crises, my Parkinson's diagnosis, and more. Through the darkness of these and other experiences, there has been enough of the light to keep us on the Way as promised to all saints.

Elizabethtown College for nearly three decades has given me space to engage in my church-related research and practice of ministry. Across four college administrations, I have been blessed by the same support and encouragement, without which I would not have been able to "pastor" as a minister and "profess" as a teacher at the same time. In keeping with what I have always experienced, the College has supported and promoted the podcast "A Church Dismantled—A Kingdom Restored" and has publicized my efforts widely. The College has also given me a sabbatical for the fall of 2021 to continue writing and publishing my work.

Keith Yoder of Teaching the Word Ministries has written the Foreword and has been a kind of "Gandalf" for Heidi and me in the past ten years of ministry. He has so often seen a different reality than we saw. Keith has spoken blessing time and again over us. He has built our confidence in ministry and in our gifts. He has seen light where we could only see darkness. More than anyone else in the past ten years, Keith has attended to our shared ministry as a couple, believing in us when we were beyond believing in ourselves.

Our congregation at Elizabethtown Mennonite Church has graciously been a space for me over the last decade to hone my preaching and writing for an audience that lives and labors in the everyday world of work, home, and play.

Dan Mast of Masthof Press and his staff have been a valued collaborator on this project—I cannot imagine a more supportive publishing partner than Dan and his team. And I am so grateful for the careful proofreading of Linda Boll.

All of these essays were written during the Covid-19 pandemic. For the most part, I have sought to retain the present tense in which they were initially penned. This book and the podcast episodes that preceded it have represented the intersection and integration of various areas of my professional and personal life that had been disparate entities in the past. They have allowed me to draw upon nearly three decades of teaching sociology, thirty-five years of sociological research, fifteen years of church and denominational consulting, twenty years of ministry, my childhood and coming-of-age in a conservative Mennonite-Amish community, my life-long struggle with the terror of God's wrath exacerbated by Obsessive-Compulsive Disorder, and the diagnosis, four years ago, of Parkinson's disease.

As you will read throughout the chapters of this book, the Parkinson's diagnosis has been a challenging but transformative experience for me. Uncannily, it has represented my own dismantling while I have been writing about the dismantling of the church. But as you will hear me say repeatedly, this disease has given me a timeline and horizon that I had not seen so clearly before. It has brought with it an encounter of the love of God, a re-conversion to Jesus, and an outpouring of his Spirit in ways I had never experienced previously in my life. And it has led to freedom, clarity of identity, and a sense of contentment like none I had known before. As I have often said, if it finally took Parkinson's disease to bring these gifts to me, then thanks be to God! For it may just be that these graces also ensure that I find my way finally "home." My prayer is that my reflections throughout this book and those yet to come in future volumes will be an encouragement to you and that they will cast a bit of light on your own journey toward the new heaven and new earth that are just beyond the horizon ahead of us.

So, accompanied by the gracious words of the apostle Paul, himself plagued by weakness and troubled with a thorn in the flesh that God would not remove, may you receive my words, like Paul's, as a means of encouragement. For amid the dismantling, "We do not lose heart. Even though our outer nature is wasting away, our inner nature is being renewed day by day. For this slight momentary affliction is preparing us for an eternal weight of glory beyond all measure, because we look not at what can be seen but at what cannot be seen; for what can be seen is temporary, but what cannot be seen is eternal" (2 Cor 4:16-18).

-Conrad L. Kanagy, Elizabethtown, PA
October 6, 2021

READERS' RESOURCES:
The website www.achurchdismantled.com contains resources to support the material in this
book, including a short video in which I address
each of the sections of the book and study guides
for personal or group reflection and discussion.
Readers may subscribe at the website to receive
weekly blog posts and "A Church Dismantled"
series updates.

PART ONE

FINDING MY WAY
THROUGH THE DARK

CHAPTER 1

I've Already Found That Fountain—
and Darkness Is Not Sin
March 16, 2021

For the last several weeks, as I've met with the Lord each morning, I've been listening to one of my favorite old hymns entitled "There Is a Fountain Filled with Blood."

> There is a fountain filled with blood drawn from Immanuel's veins. And sinners plunged beneath that flood, lose all their guilty stains. The dying thief rejoiced to see that fountain in his day. And there may I, though vile as he, wash all my sins away. E'er since by faith, I saw the stream thy flowing wounds supply, redeeming love has been my theme and shall be till I die. When this poor lisping, stammering tongue lies silent in the grave, then in a nobler, sweeter song, I'll sing Thy power to save.[2]

A recent blog post about my life-long struggle with Obsessive Compulsive Disorder and the accompanying torment over sin, shame, and guilt elicited this response from a reader:

> Step number one is to turn towards Jesus, admitting that you are a sinner. In a scenario where a doctor has diagnosed your sin as a disorder, it seems to me that repentance would

---

[2]   https://www.hymnal.net/en/hymn/h/1006.

be impossible. Thus your continued and distressing concerns of sin and guilt. Victory over your "disorder," along with the associated guilt, is immediate and lasting through faith in the finished work of Christ. I highly recommend it.

This reader's reaction gave me a chance to utter Jesus' words on the cross: "Father, forgive them, for they know not what they do [or say]." It also allows me to respond to a church that for far too long has assumed that those of us who struggle with mental illness of all kinds are weaker than others, do not have enough faith, are walking in some sort of sin, or are under the influence of some form of demonic power.

What the church for too long has failed to understand is that on some occasions, it is the church and its failures to articulate the Good News of Jesus that has been the same incubator within which depression, fear, anxiety, panic, and mental torment are nurtured and then discounted and minimized. Religious toxicity does not emerge in a vacuum. It is too often the church that has caused or at least contributed to the pain that some have lived within—the trauma out of which our disorders can grow.

Which I think is why I love this hymn so much by William Cowper from the mid-18th century. Cowper was a friend of John Newton, who of course penned "Amazing Grace," and written by one who clearly knew of what he spoke. Cowper suffered all of his life from depression, experienced a panic attack as he interviewed for a prestigious job, and attempted to take his life three times because he thought God told him to do so. He would eventually die, at least in part, for reasons related to his life-long struggle.[3]

But in the midst of one of his depressive bouts, Cowper penned the beautiful words of this hymn: "There is a fountain filled

3   https://www.umcdiscipleship.org/resources/history-of-hymns-there-is-a-foun-tain-filled-with-blood.

with blood, drawn from Immanuel's veins, and sinners plunged beneath that flood, lose all their guilty stains." Only one who was desperate for wholeness could write such words. They could not have been written by a publican or a Pharisee or even by some folks who show up for church these days. They are written by one who knows they are broken, who knows they are crooked, who knows they are desperate, and who knows just how sick they are. And these words were written precisely by one of those for whom our Savior came and for whom he comes still.

In John 9, Jesus heals a blind man. Those who stood by watching assumed that either the man or his parents had sinned. Jesus cut short their self-righteous blame game and said, "There *ain't* nobody sinned!" Instead, "this happened so that the works of God might be displayed in him." (John 9:3 NIV) And then Jesus healed the man. And as still happens far too often today, the church refused to believe and threw out the one who had been healed just as they would soon throw out the prophet who had healed the man.

But as my spiritual director reminds me, when I find myself living in shame because of criticism or discontent among the saints, "Conrad, the church is not Jesus." And so, at the end of the story, Jesus finds the man freed from his blindness but rejected by the church. Jesus reaches out to him, has coffee with him, speaks love to his wounded heart, and brings salvation not only to his body but also to his soul.

I am not ashamed to say that I have struggled with mental health issues related mainly to OCD and its accompanying cousins of depression and anxiety. Nor am I ashamed to say that I have sought the help of healing professionals time and time again. And most of all, I am not ashamed to say that like William Cowper, I've also found that fountain which flows not from the church, but from the One who was broken just like me, wounded just like me, busted just like me, and rejected just like me. And for this reason, he knows what it is like to be one of us—and why he will never stop seeking the sick, the lame, the cast-aways, the mentally ill, and just about everyone else living on the edges of their society. Why? Because he has so much more in common with them than with those who do not know they need a doctor.

In Mark 5, Jesus heals the Gerasene demoniac who had haunted the tombs with his rage, howls, and self-harm. But Jesus delivers him and sends his demons fleeing over the cliffs into the sea, embodied within a herd of swine. But rather than rejoice, those who witnessed this miracle of freedom and restoration begged Jesus to leave their region. Why? Who knows for sure? But the fact that this man's demons had been exorcised may have meant that the crowd too had begun to consider their own demons and the possible consequences of being set free. For freedom brings uncertainties, problems, questions, and disruption, and sometimes it is easier to remain bound up in our chains and hang out with our demons. And easier to ask Jesus to leave our church.

In Mark 6, Jesus comes to his hometown of Nazareth, only to find that the hometowners wanted nothing to do with him. Who was this Jesus anyway, other than a carpenter's son and the brother of James, Judas, and others? What exceptional pedigree did Jesus have? What education? And so, Mark records that because of their unbelief, Jesus was able to do only a few miracles among his family and friends.

I wonder how many of us, struggling with our demons, simply wander away from a church that, even when we are healed or freed, prefers to see us in our chains, all the while singing "Oh How I Love Jesus" and "Amazing Grace" and "Blessed Assurance" and on and on. It is one thing to declare the Good News and another thing altogether to allow that Good News to take root in our town and our church. Choosing to live in the darkness is the one sin that cannot be forgiven.

CHAPTER 2

A Letter to My Eighteen-Year-Old Self—
There Will Always Be Enough Light
February 22, 2021

> But now thus says the Lord,
> he who created you, O Jacob,
> he who formed you, O Israel:
> Do not fear, for I have redeemed you;
> I have called you by name, you are mine.
> When you pass through the waters, I will be with you;
> and through the rivers, they shall not overwhelm you;
> when you walk through the fire, you shall not be burned,
> and the flame shall not consume you. (Isaiah 43:1-2)

Dear 18-year-old self,

I want you to know that whatever you face and whatever you experience—there will always be enough Light, that these words from Isaiah are true, the most profound Truth there is.

When as a sophomore at Wheaton College, you find yourself lost in the darkness of a rain forest, walking upstream through chest-high flood waters in Papua New Guinea—there will be enough Light.

When the torment of OCD—through all your childhood and into your adult life—convinces you day after day and night after night that hell is your destiny—there will be enough Light.

7

When you and Heidi are told that she will miscarry Jacob and that you just need to go home to wait for this to happen—there will be enough Light.

When you become aware that your young marriage is breaking up in a community where good people don't experience such things and where no one knows what to say to you—there will be enough Light.

When after you and Heidi separate, you must make a decision about whether to continue into a Ph.D. program or not—and choose to do so because you have no other options with a Master's degree in Rural Sociology, there will be enough Light.

When you and Heidi must make decisions about reuniting your marriage after more than two years of separation—and marital struggles remain, there will be enough Light.

When you and Heidi and Jacob reunite in Hershey, PA, and you have applications for a teaching job out all over the country, but no leads and no interviews and no offers—there will be enough Light.

When within months of moving back together, Elizabethtown College suddenly has an opening and offers you a temporary, one-year position—there will be enough Light.

When you are asked to lead Elizabethtown Mennonite Church while also in a tenure-track position—there will be enough Light.

When within months of your ordination, you are diagnosed with papillary thyroid cancer that will persist for three years through multiple surgeries and radioactive iodine treatments—there will be enough Light.

When within months of the diagnosis, there is an initiative calling for your resignation at the church—there will be enough Light.

When Heidi is diagnosed with ovarian cancer and you both are faced with the terror of what appears to be a death sentence—there will be enough Light.

When you and Heidi are called back to ministry together when you had always said it was God's grace that led you away after your first five-year stint—there will be enough Light.

When you slide off the cedar shingle roof of your home, looking up at the sky alone and with a broken hip—there will be enough Light.

When a year later you are diagnosed with salivary gland cancer, followed by surgery and radiation treatments—there will be enough Light.

When you begin to tremor two years later and hear the specialist at Penn Medical Center say that "there is no alternative diagnosis to Parkinson's Disease,"—there will be enough Light.

When what you will experience gives you a view of a landscape hidden from others, just remember that this "is your story and this is your song," and it will always be yours to sing. And sing it you must.

And finally, remember that when you walk through the water and the fire for the last time—the Light that was always enough in the past will become the Light that embraces you and welcomes you Home.

CHAPTER 3

The Light of Pap Renno's Last Smile
August 31, 2020

When I visited my grandfather, "Pap" Erie Renno at Lewistown Hospital in the Fall of 2007, I was pretty sure that it would be our last visit. Pap was alert and smiling, talkative as usual, but his heart was failing him, and we knew his days were numbered. My last memory is of that unforgettable warm smile of Pap's as I said goodbye and walked out the door.

Pap was known widely throughout the Mennonite Church in the mid-20th century. In the tenth grade, he had dropped out of high school to stay home and help with the farm, his father having died when Pap was just a teenager. But one day in the field, Pap heard God speak his name, sharing with him that he would be called into ministry.

Eventually, that day would come, and Pap was ordained at Locust Grove Mennonite Church in Belleville, PA, serving for several decades. But he also ministered broadly across the church. He was frequently called into congregations to mediate conflicts. He served on the Mission Board of Rosedale Mennonite Missions. He was invited to speak in communities when a whole week of "revival meetings" was the norm. It is not unusual still, thirteen years after his death at eighty-eight, to hear folks around the broader church expressing warm memories of Pap.

As one of Pap's grandchildren, I remember him for many things, particularly for our frequent family gatherings. When we showed up to visit, he was always happy to see us—breaking into an exuberant grin. He frequently told me how grateful he was that I was following Jesus and serving the church. His standard answer to troubles and difficulties was, "We can trust Jesus." And before we would leave extended family gatherings, he almost always requested that we sing together "Jesus, loves me this I know, for the Bible tells me so. Little ones to him belong, they are weak, but he is strong. Yes, Jesus loves me, yes Jesus loves me, yes Jesus loves me. The Bible tells me so." Pap loved to sing this simple song despite his inability to carry a tune. But he didn't care, for this song obviously explained that smile I will never forget. I've often prayed for the kind of simple faith in and intimacy with Jesus that I saw in Pap. His was the most authentic and richest expression of piety I've ever witnessed.

Pap had known many challenges and difficulties. Called away during World War II from his young family to serve in a Civilian Public Service camp as a conscientious objector, struggling to be a successful farmer while also in the ministry, losing his oldest son to cancer, serving at a time when pastors were never expected to ask questions about self-care or were encouraged to set boundaries around their personal lives and families. And yet, he smiled.

One of Pap's frequently expressed regrets was that he had dropped out of high school as a teenager. He never seemed to forgive himself for that, and I always got the sense that he felt his ministry was inferior because of his educational status. I tried to convince him otherwise, but I'm not sure that I ever really got through. To hear Pap preach and speak, one would have had no idea that he had never completed high school. His office was packed with books from floor to ceiling—he read and studied voraciously and was as highly educated as any church leader I've known. With little formal training, he was not intimidated by this perceived deficit, even if he did regret it.

I sometimes looked at Pap as he grew older and wondered what it would be like to know that one's years were numbered—that he would not live to see some of his grandchildren and great-grandchildren grow up. What was it like to see the horizon of one's life ahead, knowing that it was coming sooner rather than later? How did he live with the knowledge of his pending death while also living fully in the moment with that smile on his face? I'm sure I wondered this about other folks, but I especially remember pondering it about Pap. I think, because he always seemed to be so content.

Which reminds me of the words of the Apostle Paul, who said, "for I have learned to be content with whatever I have." (Philippians 4:11b) Paul wrote these words near the end of his life. Paul had learned to be content the closer he got to the horizon of his life, the nearer he came to completing the race that Christ had set out before him. He became, it seems, more and more comfortable with the idea of his death, even looking forward to it with anticipation. Paul did so not with suicidal ideations—but out of the knowledge that what lay ahead would be so much grander than the momentary circumstances regardless of whether he was eating dry bread in prison or a gourmet meal in Rome or Ephesus. It just didn't matter—he was confident that what was coming on the horizon was a new heaven and new earth. When Christ called him home, he would be more than ready. "To live is Christ and to die is gain" is how that old saint put it.

Which reminds me of the line from the Heidelberg Catechism: "What is your only comfort in life and in death? That I am not my own, but belong—body and soul, in life and in death—to my faithful Savior Jesus Christ."[4] It seems that God has a way of preparing the saints for their death, but only as they also learn that God is their comfort in this life. This God, who, as the saints remind us

4   http://www.heidelberg-catechism.com/en/lords-days/1.html.

again and again, is full of compassion and holds us in the safety and security of God's womb.

My diagnosis of Parkinson's disease has helped me to understand how Pap lived with such enthusiasm, passion, warmth, hope, and a smile that expressed all of that—because at some point, he had become honest with himself about the day of his death. For it is only as we acknowledge and are open to the day of our death that we can be fully open to the days of our living. In fact, we know from the literature on aging that happiness and life satisfaction can be illustrated by a U-curve. In the decades of one's 20-40s, life satisfaction declines but in the 50s and 60s, it begins to turn upward and increase. Why? Because as we age, most of us, in one way or another, start to deal with and accept the aging process and the limitations that it brings, and we choose to make the best of the days that remain.

As I told my students last week, Parkinson's Disease has given me a new view of the horizon of my life that I would never have gotten so early, and keeping my eyes on that horizon has caused not dread but joy. I now know what I want to do with my life and what I don't want to do. I'm not going to spend time on committees that do nothing. I'm not going to say yes to going out to lunch with those who just want to flatter me with empty praise or flatten me with criticism. No, I'm going to spend whatever good days I have with my dear wife and best friend, with my son and daughter-in-law and grandsons, with genuine friends, and with my students whom I so enjoy.

What does all of this have to do with a dismantled church? A lot, I think. If the church would begin to be more comfortable with our increased marginalization in American society, with our loss of status and authority and presence, even with the declines in participation and attendance, if we began to recognize that the horizon for the church as we've known and constructed it is fast approaching, that the death of the church as we've known it has already occurred in many places throughout our country and is accelerating, we might just stop trying to cling to the safety and security promised by one politician after another seeking our vote. We might stop trying to emulate the culture that is quickly absorbing us, we might actually begin to live like the Jesus of the New Testament taught us to live, and we might be more willing to give up our lives than to gain the whole world.

What if the church simply acknowledged that God's Spirit is deconstructing us because we have failed God's mission and began to ask how God wants to use a dismantled church? What are his purposes for a dismantled church? How does he want to lead you and me into greater fruitfulness in a dismantled church?

A marginal position is a position from which the church has always been most alive and most vital and the position from which the church has most clearly seen God's reality and purposes and truth. Rather than denying our reality or working so hard to prevent what is inevitable, what if we helped the Spirit dismantle what is broken and deteriorating in the church, and like Paul, learned to be content whether in prison or in the buffet line? What if we began to embrace the coming horizon where the restored Kingdom lies just over the other side?

I suspect if we did so, the last thing that people might remember of us is our smile!

CHAPTER 4

From the Darkness of Grace as "Unmerited Favor" to the Light of a "Grace We Deserve"

May 3, 2021

Yesterday I preached a sermon entitled "Getting the Grace We Deserve," and in doing so, challenged the flawed definition of grace as "unmerited favor." It was hard to tell how this revised teaching on grace was received. Still, I recognized afterward how much I had been impacted by the 19th-century Scottish poet, novelist, and preacher George MacDonald, who was perhaps the most significant influence upon C. S. Lewis.

In one of his quotes, MacDonald describes the deep acceptance of God for us:

> Therefore, with angels and archangels, with the spirits of the just made perfect, with the little children of the kingdom, yea, with the Lord himself, and for all them that know him not, we praise and magnify and laud his name in itself, saying "Our Father." We do not draw back for that we are unworthy, nor even that we are hard-hearted and care not for the good. For it is his childlikeness that makes him God and Father. The perfection of his relation to us swallows up our imperfections, all our defects, all our evils; for our childhood is born of his fatherhood. That man [or woman] is perfect in faith who can come to God in the utter dearth of his feelings and his desires,

and without a glow or an aspiration, with the weight of low thoughts, failures, neglects, and wandering forgetfulness, and say to him, "You are my refuge, because you are my home."[5]

And then I awoke this morning to the hymn "There's a Wideness in God's Mercy," written by Frederick Faber in 1854 in England. Faber had grown up Anglican and was influenced by the hymns of the Wesley brothers as well as William Cowper, whose story I discussed previously, who in struggling with depression and anxiety, penned "There is a Fountain Filled with Blood."

Lyrics from Faber's hymn reflect the message that I preached yesterday, a revision of the view of grace so often taught in the contemporary church. I suggested that everything about Jesus' life and teaching revealed that we actually deserve God's grace and mercy from God's perspective. That as those made in God's image, God believed we were worth rescuing, thought we were a valuable treasure that he couldn't wait to hold in his arms again, believed that we are worthy of his incredible love:

> There's a wideness in God's mercy, like the wideness of the sea.
> There's a kindness in God's justice, which is more than liberty.
> There is welcome for the sinner, and more graces for the good.
> There is mercy with the Savior, there is healing in his blood.
> But we make God's love too narrow by false limits of our own,
> and we magnify its strictness with a zeal God will not own.
> For the love of God is broader than the measures of the mind,
> and the heart of the Eternal is most wonderfully kind.
> If our love were but more simple, we should rest upon God's word,
> and our lives would be illumined by the presence of our Lord.[6]

---

5   George MacDonald, *Creation in Christ* (Wheaton, IL: Harold Shaw Publishers, 1976).
6   https://hymnary.org/text/theres_a_wideness_in_gods_mercy.

What I love about this hymn is the wideness of God's love that it presents. Friends, I need a wide love, for I fall off the wagon far too often for anything otherwise. I sometimes hear some version of the following in the church: "The Christian life is about walking a fine line—not getting too carried away with this grace thing and not getting too caught in legalism. It's about balancing between." I walked that fine line for five decades, and I can't do it anymore. In a sobriety test, I've become too intoxicated with God's love to believe that I can negotiate that line successfully, nor do I think that God expects me to live in such bondage.

No, I'm going to jump whole hog into the side of grace, wallowing in it from now until the day I see my Savior face to face. So if you want to walk that tightrope trying to balance between legalism and grace, I will be praying that you lose your balance and join me in the deep end that I've fallen into. Now that I've landed in the grace that God saw me so deserving of, I'm not going anywhere. For I who was dead have come to life. I who was blind, can now see. I, who was in bondage, have found freedom. I, who was lost, have finally come home.

This is also why I so love Judson Cornwall's take on Isaiah 40:3-5 that we are building a grand and broad highway for others to find the love and compassion and glory of God for themselves. But doing so must mean that we undo some things we believe about how one comes to God and why God wants us to experience his grace. Of an emotional breakdown and crisis in his life, Cornwall says this:

> My highest ministries were being exploded into rubble, but a highway was being built right into the presence of God. My "heights" of ability and strength of ministry had become an insurmountable barrier to their getting to God. So God re-

duced me to tears while bringing them through to His presence. Let the high places go. Of course, those exalted ridges must come down! Those doctrinal highs, those experiential highs, those emotional elevations...[7]

Judson promotes the idea, using different language, that the Spirit must dismantle us as individuals and our church if we are ever going to become useful in God's grand excavation project of lowering mountains, raising valleys, making rough places a plain and crooked places straight. And some of that dismantling includes a theology of a stingy God who only begrudgingly came to earth to repair me, restore me, redeem me, and call me home again. And until this is good news for me, it won't be good news for the world in which my students freely identify with what they call "religious trauma," trauma brought on by teaching them that they were sinners and worthy of damnation before anyone ever got around to telling them that God formed them in their mother's womb, that God saw them deserving of his love and grace, and that God is still calling them back to himself and the joy of being deeply loved by Father, Son, and Holy Spirit.

---

[7]   Judson Cornwall, *Freeway Under Construction by Order of Isaiah 40:3-5* (Plainfield, NJ: Logos), 24.

CHAPTER 5

Light Shed on the Secrets of Grand-pap Byler and the Darkness of Martyrs' Mirror

December 18, 2020

For some reason, at least for a few Christmas Eve evenings during my childhood, my father would announce that he and my brothers and I were going "up the valley" to visit our Amish great-grandfather, John Byler. Quite honestly, it was about the only time of the year when I actually interacted with my great-grandfather. His daughter Rachel, my grandmother, had thirteen children of her own, my father was the oldest, so perhaps it was that family gatherings were already big enough without including that next generation of kin. Whatever the case, it was not the most exciting way to spend the night before Christmas from my childhood perspective. Grand-pap Byler was quiet and stoic, with a long white beard, and I rarely ever talked directly to him. While Aunt Sadie was always warm and engaging, it just felt a little awkward to me since we didn't visit on evenings other than Christmas Eve.

In any event, however, my dad always seemed to enjoy the evening. So I would settle down with *Martyrs' Mirror*, a thick and heavy book from the 17th century written about the centuries of saints who had in so many gruesome ways suffered at the hands of European persecutors.[8] While the book began with the martyrdom

---

[8] Thielman J. van Braught and Joseph F. Sohm, *The Bloody Theater or Martyrs' Mirror* (Scottdale, PA: Herald Press, 1987, 15th ed.).

of Jesus' disciples, most stories, in a book where deaths are illustrated by graphic prints and described in gory detail, were of my ancestors, the early Anabaptists. For in choosing to reject infant baptism, the power of the sword, allegiance to the state, and to live as Jesus had instructed and lived, many indeed significantly suffered and sacrificed life and limb.

The book, I was told as a child in my baptism instruction class, was written to remind Mennonite young people—like myself—of the sacrifice of their ancestors for the sake of Christ and as a model and expectation for Anabaptist youth—like myself—who might be considering an excursion from their historic faith, especially by joining the military. So on Christmas Eve, in the dim light of my great-grandfather's home, as I anticipated that string puppet or race track or new baseball glove that would make it hard for me to go to sleep, I also imagined a life where I might be faced with the choice of my allegiance to Christ and the consequence of living or dying depending on my choice. Even as a young child, I knew that the expectation flowing through our history was that the choice would be death.

Eventually, we wrapped up the visit and headed home, still excited about the following day but also wondering when I might be faced with that choice of life or death that just might lie ahead of me. What I didn't know about my great-grandfather in those days and would only learn later was that he had had a severe struggle with alcoholism earlier in his life. While I grew up knowing that alcohol was strictly off-limits as a possible way to spend Christmas Eve or any other eve, I didn't understand until my dad one day revealed what I had never heard anyone talk about before. For Great-grandpap's illness had clearly left pain in its wake, and silence had followed.

Decades later, when I was presenting a paper in a public setting, a stranger approached me and asked, "Are you John Byler's great-grandson?" "I am," I said. The stranger went on to tell me that he had worked as a hired man on my great-grandfather's farm, and one day in a rage of drunkenness, Grandpap Byler had chased him with a pitch fork through the barn and into the hay mow from which the young man jumped, landed on his wrists, and broke both of them. Then the stranger walked away. In all of my years, those are the only two stories I ever heard of this darker side of my great-grandfather, and I'm thankful Dad had given me a heads up before this stranger told me his story.

But I think back to the quiet stoicism of Great-grandpap Byler now and the burden of living in a culture where the model of faithfulness is portrayed in a book of martyrs, who, if we knew more about them, undoubtedly had their own dark sides and secrets. In some ways, *Martyrs' Mirror* is an old Instagram feed of the best of the saints and of what faithfulness to Christ looks like. I'm not debating their sainthood. I only know this: there was only one perfect martyr, and he showed up on Christmas Eve so I would not have to live with the weight of perfection upon me and that his righteousness would become mine regardless of who I was or what I had done!

The list of saints in the book of Hebrews includes some scoundrels with dark sides for whom alcoholism was just the beginning of failures. And I also wonder how living in the shadow of *Martyrs' Mirror* created shame for those who turned to the bottle for whatever reason. All of us, if we are honest, at one time or another, turn to something other than the One who came to receive us just as we were on that first Christmas Day. Living in the shadow of martyrs can be a pretty dark shadow and a reasonably high bar to aspire toward—enough to potentially lead any of us who recognize that we can't attain that standard to drink away our guilt and pain and shame.

I wish I had had a chance to ask Great-grandpap Byler whether he had ever been able to get beyond the shame of failed expectations in a community where failure was so often covered up or denied.

To receive forgiveness from those around him, including that young hired man who had grown old with the pain of those broken wrists? Most of all, did he ever come to accept that the Child who came at Christmas had forgiven and forgotten all? Had he moved out of the shadow of unreal expectations cast upon him by a culture that, in trying to encourage discipleship, had perhaps created despair? While quiet, Grandpap did have a thin smile that every now and then showed through. I will hope for now it was a smile of one who had come to peace with the darkness of the bottle that had haunted him as well as perhaps that book of martyrs.

And one day, I will ask him—not in the shadow of shame and condemnation but in the light of a bright new day where martyrs and those who never quite saw themselves as martyr material, will gather round the throne of the Lamb who came as a child for Grandpap Byler, for you, for me, and for all of the world that God so loved and so loves still.

PART TWO

OUT OF THE
DARKNESS

CHAPTER 6

It All Began in the Darkness
November 28, 2020

In the beginning, when God created the heavens and the earth, the earth was a formless void, and darkness covered the face of the deep, while a wind from God swept over the face of the waters. Then God said, "'Let there be light,' and there was light. And God saw that the light was good, and God separated the light from the darkness. God called the light Day, and the darkness he called Night. And there was evening, and there was morning, the first day." (Genesis 1: 1-5)

It all began in the darkness. There was no light. As I write this morning and as the year of 2020 has progressed, the darkness seems to have intensified. What began as so abstract and distant, a virus coming out of Wuhan, China, now has come so close. The home of my growing up, Big Valley, PA, had long avoided this virus. Tucked between the mountains, safe and secure, Heidi and I would go home to visit Mom and Dad earlier in the year, and it always felt like another planet. Virus, masks, social distancing, closing churches, gyms, restaurants, and bars? Not so much. We felt like we could escape all of the bad news we were hearing by getting away to a place where the darkness had not yet come.

But it has come, and with a vengeance—so close to home that it has visited both of my parents, and my dear mom, in particular, is now suffering the effects of a virus that so many had said was, well, just a hoax. But the darkness is so often like that for us. We usually can't see its descent, or we simply refuse to acknowledge its presence. For we struggle to imagine shadows that we've not seen before, darkness we've not experienced before—perhaps because we were created in the light and not the dark and maybe because we were made for the light and not the darkness.

Genesis 1 clarifies that it all began in the darkness amidst emptiness, the formlessness of the deep. But for whatever reason, on one particular day, on what would become the first of all days, God had enough of the dark. Looking out upon the world, the One who was light must have desired to bring his shining beam to the darkest of places. And so, in the beginning, the first action of God was to create light, or rather I suspect to simply bring his light to bear upon the great darkness, and in the process to separate the darkness from light. And the light of God has been intervening with and entering the darkness ever since.

Interestingly, God did not rid the planet of darkness—I wonder if he ever regrets that now. Did God know how much the night would continue to cast its shadow over our lives and the earth? Did God know then that the man and woman he was about to create would soon choose darkness over light, deception over truth, death over life? Did God know that the night would one day become so intense that he would have to intervene in such a costly way by swooping down into the darkness himself to find and rescue us?

I don't know. But on this day, and for good reason, God celebrated the light and called it good. And in doing so was simply reaffirming that he was good and that his good light had overcome the darkness. I wonder if God knew that it would be a full-time job over the next thousands of years to bring light into the darkness we would choose again and again and again. That we who would be created in the light would so often decide to go back to the darkness from which it all began. And choose darkness we continue to do—deception and lies over truth, shame and condemnation over forgiveness and grace, death over life.

Nonetheless, the promise of that beginning in Genesis is that the darkness will not last, the night will not win, the virus will not be permanent, the chaos around the current election will someday be just a footnote. The darkness that was overcome on that first day continues to and will finally be overwhelmed by the Light that dawns upon us still.

CHAPTER 7

And So God Began Again
November 29, 2020

In the beginning was the Word, and the Word was with God, and the Word was God. He was in the beginning with God. All things came into being through him, and without him not one thing came into being. What has come into being in him was life, and the life was the light of all people. The light shines in the darkness, and the darkness did not overcome it. There was a man sent from God, whose name was John. He came as a witness to testify to the light, so that all might believe through him. He himself was not the light, but he came to testify to the light. The true light, which enlightens everyone, was coming into the world... And the Word became flesh and lived among us, and we have seen his glory, the glory as of a father's only son, full of grace and truth. (John 1:1-5, 14)

When I was just a kid, I memorized the poem, *The Creation*, by James Weldon Johnson. My mother, who loved poetry, had suggested that I memorize this poem for our school talent festival. It is a remarkable piece, so clearly God-inspired and so full of light. Written in the form of an African-American sermon, Weldon's poem bursts with the kind of energy that the creation itself exploded with on that first day, for despite all of the efforts of white folks to keep Black folks down, the creative power of God within these brothers and sisters, like James Weldon Johnson, could never be contained and would one day—with the help of God himself—shatter through the darkness of white supremacy and institutional racism. In fact, this movement would be led by a group of Black pastors who could no longer accept the status quo regardless of the cost to their bodies and livelihoods. Like God himself on that first day of creation, these pastors who led the civil rights movement refused to give darkness the last word.

As it turns out, James Weldon Johnson was himself an African-American activist who would come to lead the national office of the NAACP. But how could such an inspired piece not be written by one who so clearly knew what it was to live within the darkness and shadows of Jim Crow, shadows created by those who claimed to be children of the Light even while serving the author of darkness? White folks who were the children of the generations before them, of parents and grandparents who took upon themselves the task of separating Black from white, and what they perceived to be light from dark, good from bad, and human from that which was assumed to be less so. How strange that so many who called themselves Christians would embrace this apartheid that was so obviously from the pit of hell itself. This tragic history, and the consequences that continue into the present, reminds us once again that we who were created in the light so often choose to impose darkness on others, but at the same time fail to recognize that darkness can only be imposed upon others by those who are in the darkness themselves.

Those who embraced Jim Crow as God's divine plan and who celebrated lynchings on Saturday before going to church on Sunday, remind us that we are all capable of failing to see that while we think we are children of light, we are actually those who have chosen the darkness. But as is so often the case, it is among those upon whom we impose our darkness that the light again emerges to remind us of our own dimness. It is so often among those we oppress that freedom breaks through to remind us how bound up and imprisoned we are. It is often among those we thought blind that sight and truth and revelation come forth to remind the rest of us that we who thought we saw the light are those most in the dark.

But the eternally great and undeniably good news is that the light of the first day of creation cannot be overcome by even humanity's best efforts to destroy it. In the end, the One who created light and the Word that was with the light on that first day are relentless. Light still shows up in the most unlikely and in the darkest of places. How little we know about the light.

Besides *The Creation* and other poems, James Weldon Johnson is also the author of what is often called the African-American national anthem—a hymn full of the kind of light that only one who has had to live in darkness, but did not allow the darkness to overcome him, could write:

> Lift ev'ry voice and sing
> 'Til earth and heaven ring
> Ring with the harmonies of Liberty
> Let our rejoicing rise
> High as the list'ning skies
> Let it resound loud as the rolling sea
> Sing a song full of the faith that the dark past has taught us
> Sing a song full of the hope that the present has brought us
> Facing the rising sun of our new day begun
> Let us march on 'til victory is won
> God of our weary years
> God of our silent tears
> Thou who has brought us thus far on the way
> Thou who has by Thy might
> Led us into the light
> Keep us forever in the path, we pray

Lest our feet stray from the places, our God,
where we met Thee
Lest our hearts drunk with the wine of the world,
we forget Thee
Shadowed beneath Thy hand
May we forever stand
True to our God
True to our native land.[9]

In a year when the darkness at so many levels has been in the daily headlines, let us not forget when and from where this song of hope and light emerged. It came from within a darkness that was no match for the light of that first created day.

9   https://en.wikipedia.org/wiki/Lift_Every_Voice_and_Sing.

CHAPTER 8

To Whom Will You Be Light and Comfort?
November 30, 2020

Is not this the fast that I choose: to loose the bonds of injustice, to undo the thongs of the yoke, to let the oppressed go free, and to break every yoke? Is it not to share your bread with the hungry, and bring the homeless poor into your house; when you see the naked, to cover them, and not to hide yourself from your own kin? Then your light shall break forth like the dawn, and your healing shall spring up quickly; your vindicator shall go before you, the glory of the Lord shall be your rear guard. Then you shall call, and the Lord will answer; you shall cry for help, and he will say, Here I am. If you remove the yoke from among you, the pointing of the finger, the speaking of evil, if you offer your food to the hungry and satisfy the needs of the afflicted, then your light shall rise in the darkness and your gloom be like the noonday. (Isaiah 58:6-10)

Back to that poem entitled *The Creation* by James Weldon Johnson that I memorized as a kid for our school's talent festival.[10] Even just a few of its stanzas reflect the explosive energy of light that overflowed from James Weldon Johnson's soul.

---

[10] James Weldon Johnson, *God's Trombones* (New York: The Viking Press, 1927).

And God stepped out on space,
And he looked around and said:
I'm lonely—
I'll make me a world.
And far as the eye of God could see
Darkness covered everything,
Blacker than a hundred midnights
Down in a cypress swamp.
Then God smiled,
And the light broke,
And the darkness rolled up on one side,
And the light stood shining on the other,
And God said: That's good!
Then God reached out and took the light in his hands,
And God rolled the light around in his hands
Until he made the sun;
And he set that sun a-blazing in the heavens.
And the light that was left from making the sun
God gathered it up in a shining ball
And flung it against the darkness,
Spangling the night with the moon and stars.
Then down between
The darkness and the light
He hurled the world;
And God said: That's good!
Then God himself stepped down—
And the sun was on his right hand,
And the moon was on his left;
The stars were clustered about his head,
And the earth was under his feet.
And God walked, and where he trod
His footsteps hollowed the valleys out
And bulged the mountains up...

As I noted earlier, my mother directed me to this poem. As a kid who walked in so much emotional turmoil, I now wonder what her motivation was? Hope that I would discover some light for my dark journey? I am sure that it was only by her constant encouragement that I ever memorized the entire length of the piece. But in this, like every other project I attempted as a kid—from baking bread to cake decorating to memorizing poetry and on and on—Mom consistently said two things when I would get discouraged with a task and consider giving up: "Conrad," she said, "you recognize the problems with this project more than others do because you are closer to it than anyone else. Others will not see the blemishes that you see." And then she would say, "You can do this!"

Today I work with students who carry a lot of shame. Social science research shows that younger cohorts today have higher levels of narcissism than generations before them. But with narcissism comes shame because we become more focused on ourselves, both on our achievements and success but also our mistakes and failures. We are more scrutinizing about who we are and what we look like and what we are doing compared to our friends and peers on Facebook, Instagram, Snapchat, and more. When I ask my students about their higher levels of depression and anxiety than the generations before them, they quickly point to social media. That's where the success of others is constantly being displayed, where the best of those others, but not their worst, is continuously being streamed.

The problem with social media is that it lacks the context to reveal the whole of who we are and allows us a way to frame the best of our outer selves while burying the blemishes, the wounds, the pain, the insecurities—in fact, our humanity. But what my mom taught me to do was to accept that as a human being, there would be imperfections in what I created and the new things I tried. Mom empowered me—not by telling me I could do anything that I put my mind to, which only feeds narcissism and shame—but rather that I was capable of many things if I was willing to accept the imperfections that I saw in the outcome.

I often hear students offer a qualification before or after they share some answer in class like "I'm not sure this makes any sense," or "This is a stupid question," or "I don't know where I am going with this" and on and on. I've gotten to the point where I now interrupt and say, "Please do not disqualify yourself, and please do not apologize for yourself." And then I tell them the two things Mom shared with me "You see the blemishes more than others. And you can do this." For lest we give up in discouragement and wrap ourselves back up in that old blanket of shame, we all need people in our lives who will say these things to us.

I wonder what folks told James Weldon Johnson when he was doing what so many African-Americans were not doing during his day—publishing poems and hymns, leading the NAACP, and serving as an activist, educator, diplomat, and lawyer. I wonder who told James Weldon Johnson that he could achieve the many things that he did? Who gave him the confidence? Who uncovered the remarkable gifts within him?

It turns out that as he was growing up, it was his mother who encouraged him to develop interests in music and literature. As a school teacher and musician, she passed on to her sons her love of the arts—a passion that could only have been instilled in them by one who loved both the arts and her sons. But she also encouraged them to break through the barriers that lay in the path of Black folks as she became the first African-American to teach in a Florida grammar school.

As scholars, activists, and artists, the Johnson brothers' voices confronted the voices of a dominant white culture that refused to hear the truth of African-American scholars such as W.E.B. Dubois in that period. The oppressive power of racism of that time and the dehumanization of Black folks did not prevent James Weldon Johnson from meeting that oppression with the creative energy that challenged it. I wonder who told him that it didn't matter what others said but that he was created good, that blackness did not diminish his goodness, that racism did not justify oppression, that others did not define who James Weldon Johnson was or what he was capable of creating. I suspect it was the same mother who encouraged his God-given creativity and who saw the gifts of God within her sons.

For it would have been impossible, I suspect, for someone to write the words of this poem without believing in their God-given dignity and without recognizing that the power of the Creator flowed through their veins. One of James Weldon Johnson's well-known quotes is along the same lines that I tell my students: "You are young, gifted, and Black. We must begin to tell our young—there's a world waiting for you; yours is the quest that's just begun."

So just who might you know that needs to hear what Mom told me, "Don't worry about the mistakes and failures—you see them more keenly than others do. And by the way, you can do this." Who might you be called to give these words of empowerment while also claiming them for yourself?

CHAPTER 9

God in the Dark
December 17, 2020

It all began in the dark. The book of Genesis makes that clear. And over that darkness, the Spirit of God hovered, brooded, hung out. In fact, the Hebrew word for hovered suggests something like the Spirit fluttered lovingly over the chaos of the deep. And of course, it was out of that love that the light was born, light that would not be overcome by evil. Listening to evangelical theology over the decades, one gets the sense that God is incompatible with the dark, almost as if he is too weak to deal with darkness, too holy to get involved in the ugliness and messiness so often found in the dark. And so we confine God to a space far away from anything remotely human. For to be human is to live in the dark, to experience the dark, to get lost in the dark, to make our homes in the dark. On many days, to be human is to choose the dark, if only because we've never caught a glimpse of anything else. And so we create a theology of divinity vs. humanity, an angry God fed up with angry people, a God so beyond us and so out of touch with us.

But this is not the biblical story, for such a theology, if true, would never have conceived of Christmas. That God would have stayed in the heavens. That God would have started all over again with folks on some other far distant planet. The last thing that God would have done was what this God did—get dressed up in the skin of the very people we so often think he despised. No, this God had no fear of darkness, for he had hovered over it and had brought light screaming out of it. No, the last thing this God was afraid of was darkness. And the last thing this God was going to do was let the darkness win, allow that angel of death with whom he had already dueled and kicked out of heaven to have the last word.

No, this God was so unafraid of darkness that he entered into it, so fearless of the night that for a moment, he became it. So desperate to deliver his people from the darkness that he carried it for us. No, I can't accept a theology within which the God of that theology is afraid of the dark or too good for the dark or unable to enter and rescue me from it. Advent reminds us that not only were we sitting in the dark waiting for God but that God was sitting in the dark waiting for us.

CHAPTER 10

Why the Darkness Is So Hard to Comprehend But Perhaps the Light Even More So
December 1, 2020

The true Light, which enlightens everyone, was coming into the world. He was in the world, and the world came into being through him, yet the world did not know him. He came to what was his own, and his own people did not accept him. (John 1:9-11)

A year ago, while visiting the Holocaust Museum as I do each year with my students, I purchased and finally read Elie Wiesel's powerful and troubling book, *Night*.[11] It is a book that helps us understand why we often prefer to ignore the coming night and remain in the darkness of denial rather than respond to the truth of the light even when it nearly smacks us over the head.

Elie was a teenage Holocaust survivor who barely lived through the concentration camps and whose entire family died in the camps. Elie was 13 years old when he expressed a desire to learn of the deep mysteries of Kabballah, the mystical tradition of the Jewish religion. But he couldn't find anyone to teach him except for a very poor man on the margins of his Hungarian community named Moishe the Beadle. And so, he became Elie's teacher of the mysteries of God.

---

[11]   Elie Wiesel, *Night* (New York: Hill and Wang, 2006).

One day, Elie's teacher was hauled away by the Nazis and placed on a train. But the old man escaped and returned to the village of Elie and pleaded with the residents to leave ahead of the Nazi arrival. He described the atrocities he had witnessed—including the shooting of both adults and infants. But no one believed him, attributing this strange message to the fact that Moishe had always been strange. The old man grew exasperated because no one, not even Elie, believed the Germans were doing all of the dark and horrifying atrocities that Moishe had observed.

But indeed, his stories were true, and eventually, the Germans showed up in Elie's town. Given numerous opportunities to escape the coming invasion before it occurred, the people of Elie's town continued to believe and act as if such warnings were just more fake news. Sadly, as is so often the case, the despised prophet Moishe the Beadle was correct. The voices on the margins see reality, but it is their residence on the periphery that causes us to discount their version of events.

Do we ever stop to think that perhaps they've always been sidelined by others precisely because their perspective is so contrary to what the rest of us want to believe, but just may be the truth? It is hard for us to accept the light when it shows up because we have become so accustomed to the night. But being able to see in the dark does not change the fact that we are still in the shadows.

After living in the dark for so long, it seems so startling, glaring, bright when the light finally shows up. The contrast is so great that our first instinct is often to turn the light off again or to do what we can to dim that light. And so it was with the light that Christ brought to this dark planet 2000 years ago. So many ignored him. So many preferred their darkness. And so many reject him still for the very same reasons.

CHAPTER 11

The Light That Became Our Darkness Came to Free Us From That Darkness Once and For All
December 2, 2020

The Scripture records that Christ, who knew no sin, became sin for us. It also notes that Christ bore our curse—the curse of our darkness. I understand that the idea of sin and even the language of sin is not something that we are very comfortable with these days. We have connected such language to our shame, condemnation, and guilt—all things that the Enlightenment debunked in promoting the goodness of humankind and the free will of the individual. But releasing the genie of individual freedom has not solved the problem of darkness and, if anything, has only made things worse as we look around us these days.

Sin, which at its root is simply our deep separation from God and our efforts to fill in that emptiness by elevating ourselves to godlike status, keeps shedding its virus just as is Covid-19 these days. And all of our efforts to stem the spreading of the Coronavirus or our sin are just never enough to bend the curve back to the elimination of either. We who were created in the light so often choose to keep living in the darkness.

Given this tendency, God sensed that for the sake of the world "he so loved," he would have to both enter the darkness to find us and then take that darkness upon himself. And so he did. God came to us

41

in Christ not to condemn or shame us but to bring light to us. That is the point of the gospel—not that God was angry with us and so sent Jesus to save us from God's anger at us—but because God was so distressed and grieved that the darkness he had separated from the light kept coming back to haunt us. What remained incomplete about the first creation in the first beginning, God revisited in Christ. This time, he not only came to separate us from the darkness but to become the darkness so that once and for all it would be swallowed up by the light. But this would not come without cost to God. Isaiah sounds the alarm:

> Who has believed what we have heard? And to whom has the arm of the Lord been revealed? For he grew up before him like a young plant and like a root out of dry ground; he had no form or majesty that we should look at him, nothing in his appearance that we should desire him. He was despised and rejected by others; a man of suffering and acquainted with infirmity; and as one from whom others hide their faces, he was despised, and we held him of no account. Surely he has borne our infirmities and carried our diseases; yet we accounted him stricken, struck down by God, and afflicted. But he was wounded for our transgressions, crushed for our iniquities; upon him was the punishment that made us whole, and by his bruises we are healed. All we like sheep have gone astray; we have all turned to our own way, and the Lord has laid on him the iniquity of us all. (Isaiah 53:1-6)

There is nothing of condemnation in this passage—only a love that chose to enter and become the darkness, so that in the shadows, we can always know that he is with us and so that we can know our time in the dark is always temporary. When I was 12 or 13 years old, I memorized Isaiah 53 for our church Christmas program. Why this passage, I wondered? It seemed so out of place in a season when we celebrate with gifts and stockings and trees and ornaments and food and on and on. And yet, whoever organized that year's Christmas program knew exactly what they were doing, even if I didn't get it. Because there is no way to celebrate the Messiah's birth without doing so in the context of his coming death and resurrection-otherwise Christ's birth makes no sense. If the dark powers had not been overcome by the death and resurrection of our Lord, the angels on the hills and the star over Bethlehem would simply be a cruel joke! In so many ways, what we celebrate at Christmas in the coming of the baby Jesus is, in fact, the journey to the cross that he began the moment he was born. Jesus was born, feet hitting the ground, running straight for the hill of Golgotha.

I am struck by how explicitly some of the old Christmas carols name the darkness that Jesus came to deliver us from:

> God rest ye merry gentlemen,
> Let nothing you dismay,
> Remember Christ our Savior,
> Was born on Christmas Day
> To save us all from Satan's pow'r
> When we were gone astray
> Oh tidings of comfort and joy
> Comfort and joy
> Oh tidings of comfort and joy.[12]

Or…

> O come, O Branch of Jesse's stem,
> unto your own and rescue them!
> From depths of hell your people save,
> and give them victory o'er the grave.[13]

---

[12]   Unknown author, early English Christmas Carol circa 16th century.
[13]   Thomas Helmore, 1861. https://www.musixmatch.com/.

In our contemporary world that so much rejects the reality of sin and death and suffering, these old biblical realities of victory over Satan through the death and resurrection of Christ don't get much air time. But if they do not, we will either be among those who deny the reality of evil in our lives and the church and the world and allow it full reign, or we will wallow in condemnation and guilt and shame. But we will not be walking in the light as he is in the light. It is your choice and mine to make: come out of the darkness into the light or remain in the dark. But if we choose the latter, we can never say that God sent us to hell or that the devil made us do it. Here, the Enlightenment got it right—we have the free will to choose and live with the consequences now and after death.

PART THREE

PEERING THROUGH
THE DARK

CHAPTER 12

Peering Through the Dark—Knowing There Must Be Light Out There

March 23, 2021

A friend who follows my podcast recently noted that I certainly have absorbed the sociological perspective. My immediate response was something to the effect that "I think that it was always embedded within me—that I found sociology because I had always questioned the reality of the cultural context within which I grew up." I added, "In fact, I think that is how I survived."

What I meant was that the sociological perspective, which refuses to accept the "taken for granted reality" of one's world, helped me to negotiate and find my way through a cultural map with signs that often pointed to "this way to hell" and not "this way to heaven." I have no doubt that my experience of that culture was in some ways unique to who I was and to my religious preoccupation. But I've also heard from enough others to know that I was not alone in perceiving reality as such.

My students are reading Ira Wagler's second book entitled *Broken Roads: Returning to My Amish Father*.[14] Ira grew up in the Old Order Amish Church and left that culture at the age of 27, after years of torment and coming and going, but finally recognizing that he could not survive within it.[15] In this most recent memoir,

---

[14]   Ira Wagler, *Broken Roads: Returning to My Amish Father* (Tennessee: Faith-Words, 2020).
[15]   *Broken Roads*, 1.

Ira describes the reconnection he makes with his father, himself an Amish writer and founder of numerous publications and Pathway Publishers—a publisher of Amish materials.

In reflecting on his childhood, Ira notes and then asks:

> I have always felt that the fictional writings and op-eds... were less than honest. Too much gooey mush. Too didactic. Too pat. Too formulaic and predictable. All the same answers, all the time. All the loose ends are neatly tied up in a little package. Over the years, I have wondered many times if my father and his contemporaries ever questioned the path they chose. The God they served. Did they ever despair that He exists? Question their faith? Or was it always cut and dried?[16]

These are sociological questions, but they are also deeply spiritual questions. For sociology as an enterprise, in some ways, is nothing more than creating space to ask questions that others have been afraid to ask, that others have been punished for asking, that others have forgotten are even questions anymore.

One of my students noted that the Amish "formula" just didn't work for folks like Ira. The formula or equation or recipe that was meant to bring order and community, for folks like Ira brought confusion, torment, and alienation instead. And when the discomfort of the latter exceeds the comfort and promise of the former, stepping out, even if it is into an abyss, might be the first step toward home, toward salvation, toward grace, toward our Lord.

This is why I resist running too quickly from the thesis of *A Church Dismantled*. One reader noted that such a thesis is just part of the current "spirit of the age." I beg to differ—this deconstruction of darkness began the moment we sinned and separated from God

---

16   *Broken Roads*, 2.

in Eden; it continued at the Tower of Babel; it was the origin of the Protestant Reformation, and I would argue it is always the precursor to any genuine renewal movement of the Spirit.

No, the dismantling of a church that too often brought darkness rather than light to those of us peering through the night for the light is holy work. It is ongoing work. It is the excavation work of the Spirit in Isaiah 40—removing mountains, raising valleys, making rough places a plain and crooked places straight. And in the culture I grew up in should also include the dismantling of billboards with Scriptures that remind passersby of darkness rather than the light, which kept kids like me awake at night peering through that darkness, believing beyond belief that light must be out there somewhere.

It must have been one of those nights when I distinctly remember my mother teaching me Psalm 56:3, the "Psalm of the Week" for me this week: "What time I am afraid, I will trust in Thee." Despite my chronic belief that the One to be most feared was God himself, it was his grace alone that caused me to doubt that the darkness was the only reality or even the most credible reality, and to believe that out there somewhere and someday, the light would show up for me.

And thanks be to God, it did and has.

CHAPTER 13

Walking Into the Darkness
Before We Know It
March 12, 2021

Most of us have had the experience of enjoying a summer evening beneath a setting sun, only to suddenly realize we are now in the dark. Talking, reading, or whatever we were doing—night has now overtaken us. And as long as we know the way home, we aren't usually unsettled by this. We pack up, say goodbye to one another and to the day, and go home with warm memories in our hearts.

But sometimes, as night falls, we realize that we don't know the way home. What had begun gloriously suddenly becomes ominous. What seemed like streams of water and green pastures are suddenly full of shadows, unknown noises, and an awareness that we entered the valley without a plan for getting home in the dark.

I grew up in a valley, what locals call the Big Valley. Our home was situated up against the foot of Stone Mountain—the western side of the Valley. As a result, when the sun went down behind our house, the darkness fell quickly. The other side of the Valley remained fully lit—but our side was rapidly darkening.

It can be disorienting to be suddenly in the dark, to move from confidence to confusion, from fellowship to fear, from lightness of heart to heaviness. And it can all happen so quickly on a day that begins like any other. In the middle of entirely ordinary and everyday circumstances, without warning and without our awareness. And especially when everyone else seems to be walking around in the light—what is wrong with us?

Sometimes in retrospect, we recognize that we were living in a place of danger all along without knowing it. God's mercy sometimes keeps us from seeing this reality until we can handle it or until our safety is assured, or until we need to know what to do next. The Psalmist tells us that sometimes it is only in looking back that we see the footprints of God through the dark waters, footprints that led us through the danger. But I think it is also true that sometimes this recognizing occurs only after we have been walking through dangerous waters. Again, God's mercy sometimes works that way.

The Psalm I am spending time in this week is chapter 143—a psalm that so clearly speaks of the experience of night falling and the darkness pressing in on us:

> Hear my prayer, O LORD; give ear to my supplications in your faithfulness; answer me in your righteousness. Do not enter into judgment with your servant, for no one living is righteous before you. For the enemy has pursued me, crushing my life to the ground, making me sit in darkness like those long dead. Therefore my spirit faints within me; my heart within me is appalled. I remember the days of old, I think about all your deeds, I meditate on the works of your hands. I stretch out my hands to you; my soul thirsts for you like a parched land. Answer me quickly, LORD, my spirit fails. Do not hide your face from me, or I shall be like those who go down to the Pit. Let me hear of your steadfast love in the morning, for in you I put my trust. Teach me the way I should go, for to you, I lift up my soul. Save me, O LORD, from my enemies; I have fled to you for refuge. Teach me to do your will, for you are my God. Let your good spirit lead me on a level path. For your name's sake, O LORD, preserve my life. In your righteousness, bring me out of trouble. In your steadfast love, cut off my enemies, and destroy all my adversaries, for I am your servant. (Psalm 143)

I wonder where the Psalmist was when he wrote this cry. Had he known beforehand that he was walking into the darkness? Had he followed God into that dark place where the enemy crushed him to the ground? Had he walked into the night while it was still daylight and forgotten to pay attention to the sun's direction? Had he been so occupied with the calling of God that he had failed to recognize the risk he was in?

I don't know the answer. But what I do know is that sometimes, without our knowing it, God calls us to follow him into the darkness. We might even begin the journey with anticipation and excitement, but the longer we walk with God in that space, the more we face the relentless pursuit of an enemy bent on our destruction. And eventually, after enough of these assaults, our spirits indeed grow faint and our hearts dismayed. But Lord? We followed you into this place. We got here because we followed you here. But as saints do, the Psalmist remains grounded in the only One who offers safety: "Answer me quickly, O Lord.... Do not hide your face from me.... Let the morning bring me word of your unfailing love, for I have put my trust in you." As I so often have told folks in the darkness, "No matter what we are facing, the only Safe Hands are those of our Creator. There is no other alternative. Well, there is, but it is always death."

Since Saturday, I have been running a fever and experiencing various symptoms, but I have tested negative for Covid-19 twice in the last week. It has been a challenging month for Heidi and me in terms of our health. I've sometimes wondered if there isn't a connection between what I've been writing in this Lenten series and the darkness we have been experiencing this month. I don't know. But what I do know, as I told a friend this week, "I have cashed in my chips with Jesus. There ain't no way I'm turning back now."

CHAPTER 14

When What Appears as Darkness Is Just Hiding the Light
February 26, 2021

One of my favorite sociological theorists, Peter Berger, notes something to the effect that the "wisdom of sociology" is that things are so often NOT what they appear or seem to be.[17] In other words, our eyes—both physical and spiritual—often deceive us. Noah ben Shea, a favorite author of mine whose short essays about Jacob the Baker I sometimes read and discuss with my students, describes how we create walls of stones and pebbles year after year as we grow older.[18] These stones represent our experiences, biases, stereotypes, assumptions, and on and on and on. And in some cases, the walls may function to protect or comfort us, at least for a while. But as we grow older, we recognize that we no longer see the world as it is, but rather the wall we constructed. And so, as we age, some of us begin to take apart that wall so that we can see the world again. But as ben Shea notes, we won't ever see things again as we did as a child.

And for this reason, I suspect Jesus so clearly said that it would be the children, not the "wise and learned," who would see the Kingdom. I remember fifteen years or so ago reading this passage in Luke 10 and feeling cut to my heart with the realization that, up to that point in my life, so much of my energy had gone into being part of

---

[17]   Peter Berger, *Invitation to Sociology* (New York: Doubleday, 1963).
[18]   Noah ben Shea, *Jacob the Baker* (New York: Ballentine, 1990).

that community who were so clearly NOT going to see the King-dom, according to Jesus. I grieved that my efforts to build status and credentials were precisely the stones that had created the wall in front of me.

And so, in the past few years, assisted by the early onset of Parkinson's Disease and my awareness of a horizon and a river ahead, I have made an accelerated effort to take down the stones that have blocked my view of Jesus and the Kingdom of God. Of course, we can't undo these things alone, hardwired into us over the years. But as Jesus said about the rich man, all things are possible with God. I'm counting on the "all things are possible" in this season of my life.

So in this Lenten season, might one of our prayers just be that the Spirit of God would remove those stones and pebbles in our walls that have blocked us from seeing God himself as the loving and compassionate One that he is? Walls that have also stopped us from seeing others as deeply loved by God and created with God's imprint upon them? And can we go one step further and name what we see in those persons that perhaps no one else has ever bothered to name about them? That they are loved. That they have courage. That they are kind. That you appreciate their warm smile. That they work hard. That they persevere. That they are beautiful. That they are survivors. That you are glad that you know them. That they are not alone.

CHAPTER 15

UFOs or Angels?
December 4, 2020

A year ago, a former U.S. official declared that "there is compelling evidence that we [on earth] may not be alone."[19] He was referring to video footage of an unidentified flying spacecraft that, in his words, was "denying the laws of aerodynamics," had no "obvious forms of propulsion," and was "maneuvering in ways beyond…the healthy G-forces of a human or anything biological." It turns out that the Pentagon has spent over 22 million dollars just looking for these kinds of blurry images.

Consider for a moment these possible UFO sightings as compared to the incredible moment in history that Luke describes, where heavenly angels appeared to these nameless shepherds on the hillside outside Bethlehem. I don't know what the conversation among the shepherds must have been like, but I can almost hear them say: "Hey Levi, hey Shem, Abraham—I've got a sneaking suspicion that we are not alone out here tonight. I mean, just look at those angels jetting around the sky with no obvious forms of propulsion and maneuvering in ways that go far beyond G-forces any human being could handle."

Of course, there are many apparent differences between the UFO stories this week and the appearance of angels that night in

---

[19]   https://www.cnn.com/2017/12/18/politics/luis-elizondo-ufo-pentagon/index.html.

Bethlehem. First, we have to go looking for UFOs, maybe even paying 22 million dollars just for a glimpse of one. In the gospel story, we learn that God came freely looking for us. We don't need to look for God—he is always looking for us. Second, we have no idea what these UFOs are or if they exist, but Christ came at Christmas to make us fully aware of who God is; that what we see in Christ is who we understand God always to have been. The author of Hebrews describes Christ as the "radiance of God's glory and the exact representation of his being." (Hebrews 1:3, NIV) Third, we have no idea what these alleged UFOs are up to or whether they mean to heal or destroy us, but God made it clear on that night in Bethlehem that he was up to good on our behalf, he had come to restore peace to earth, to restore creation to himself. Remember what the Apostle John reminded us—that Jesus as the Word made flesh is the creative life-giving and light-giving source which came from the Father for us. And of course, this is what the prophets had foretold: "That the people walking in darkness have seen a great light and on those living in the shadow of death a light has dawned…. For to us a child is born, and to us, a Son is given." (Isaiah 9:2 and 6a, NIV)

The coming of Jesus wasn't just an earth invasion by a powerful being who wanted to put his glory on display and show off the forces of heaven that night. No, this is the story of a deeply personal God who wanted to make right all the wrongs that had for too long gotten in the way of his relationship with his children, whom he so deeply loved. This was a coming of God not to the earth in some generic sense, but a coming of God to those tired, cold shepherds on the hillside, the coming of God to Mary and Joseph, the appearance of God to Simeon and Anna in the temple who had waited decades for this day, the coming of God to foreigners from Persia whose restless hearts had kept them up many nights in anticipation of the sign of the Messiah's coming, and the coming of God to you and me.

God invaded earth, yes, but the miracle of miracles is that he invaded and continues to invade our hearts so that we are Christ-filled people. We are known for having the Christ child within us who changes everything, including the most unchangeable things. He never stops changing us, so long as we keep making room for him to lodge within us. We are never stuck in sin or darkness or fear or anxiety or death or depression. He comes to set us free—you and me. No matter how you failed this year, no matter how far you have fallen, no matter how difficult the year has been, no matter how painfully those around you have treated you, no matter how difficult the health news you have received, no matter how uncertain the future—the Christmas story reminds us that we are indeed not alone. Christ has entered the world and our darkness to redeem, forgive, give light, resurrect, restore, and make whole.

CHAPTER 16

The Happy Ones Just May Be Those in the Dark

December 8, 2020

Y et whatever gains I had, these I have come to regard as loss because of Christ. More than that, I regard everything as loss because of the surpassing value of knowing Christ Jesus my Lord. For his sake I have suffered the loss of all things, and I regard them as rubbish, so that I may gain Christ and be found in him, not having a righteousness of my own that comes from the law, but one that comes through faith in Christ, the righteousness from God, based on faith. I want to know Christ and the power of his resurrection and the sharing of his sufferings by becoming like him in his death, if somehow I may attain the resurrection from the dead. (Philippians 3:7-11)

It is essential to keep the end of one's life in view. Seeing one's future has a way of helping one to let go; to stop clutching; to stop striving; to stop performing—allows one to stop holding onto our idols so that we can be held onto by the Savior who awaits us at the end. Suffering has a way of preparing us for the end. Indeed, grief has a way of creating an anticipation of the end—not in terms of a suicidal wish but a recognition that so much of what one desires to experience on earth will only be experienced in the new heaven and new earth: family relationships that chronically create pain, conflict with others in our church community that seems unresolvable, chronic suffering (emotional, spiritual, physical, relational).

The absence of healing here only causes our souls to growl as our stomachs do so when hungry for the wholeness that awaits us. The lack of resolved relationships here only increases our desire to be held in the arms of that One who has resolved everything through his death on the cross. The absence of answers here only intensifies our heart's desires to experience the One who is the answer to all of our questions. Indeed, the suffering we experience intensifies our desire for joy.

All of these things have a way of magnifying the joy that awaits us in the new heaven and earth. They amplify the heavenly music on the hills of Bethlehem that was meant for us as much as it was for those shepherds. Suffering and difficult news remind us that we were made for wholeness and good news. For those who place their hope in the Messiah, we, like Paul, can know that our sufferings on this side of heaven are nothing compared to the glorious future that awaits us.

Charles de Foucauld says this:

> Pity those whose happiness…keeps them attached to the world. God is good and has so despoiled us of everything that we can draw our breath only by turning our heads to him. How great is his mercy, how divine his goodness, for he has torn everything away from us so that we may be more completely his. So the sufferers are the happy ones through the goodness of God. May these days of Christmas festival bring you, in your suffering, I do not say consolation, but the blessing God intends for you. The Child Jesus will perhaps not give you any sweetness—he reserves that for the weak ones—but his hands will nonetheless be spread to bless you in these days of Christ-

mastide, and whether you feel it or no, he will pour abundant grace into your soul.[20]

You see, for the saint, each experience of suffering has a kind of cumulative effect in two ways: it slowly creates the death of one's self. It causes us to cling more tightly to Jesus, and it builds anticipation of that day when every tear will be gone and when all suffering will be passed.

More days than ever before, I yearn and anticipate and am excited about seeing Jesus and experiencing the new heaven and earth where the Messiah reigns and everything has come together in him. It will be a place where the darkness has no presence to intimidate, threaten, lie, deceive, or create anxiety and fear. This is why Christmas must be connected to the cross, not in a way that diminishes the joy of Christmas and the coming of this child, but that heightens that joy. This is what happens when we are aware through this child, that the cross and thus our freedom and life and resurrection have become realities. Because of the coming of the Messiah, we have nothing to fear in life or in death—but only to rejoice with those angels, shepherds, and even the sheep: "Glory to God in the highest and on earth peace to those on whom his favor rests."

20   Charles de Foucauld, *Meditations of a Hermit* (London: Burns, Oates, and Washbourne, 1930).

CHAPTER 17

The More We Live in the Darkness, the More We Are Grateful for the Light

December 10, 2020

Christmas is probably my favorite time in the church calendar. I love Lent and Easter also, but the idea that after 400 years of silence in which time the world did not hear from heaven, and then suddenly all kinds of heavenly activity broke through—angels appearing to Zechariah, to Mary, to Joseph, to the shepherds, a star in the east that brought pagan astrologers to the Christ child, and dreams that warned of dangers. All of a sudden, the heavens broke in upon the earth in a way that had never happened before. The kingdom of God was on the move, coming to earth, coming to you and to me and to the generations that follow us.

And yet, the reality of the 400 years of silence that preceded the breakthrough of heaven to earth is sometimes more what I identify with than anything else, and I suspect that you do too if you are honest. Which, of course, is one of the beauties of the four weeks of Advent that precede the birth of Christ.

Those four weeks symbolize our own feeling of distance from God sometimes. Those weeks reflect our own hopelessness about where God is and why he seems so powerless to answer our prayers. Those weeks that represent our despair and despondency brought on by sudden news of illness or the return of test results that point to a recurrence of disease, a personal crisis in which our energy has been drained and we are left with only anger, and struggle with sexual identity that is suffered in silence out of fear of rejection if we are honest about those struggles, the chronic experience of mental illness and depression and anxiety or bipolar disorder or schizophrenia that others just do not understand, the doubts I have about whether Jesus is truly the Son of God or whether I can trust the Bible to be true, the loneliness of a life in which no one reaches out to check to see if I am okay, the memory of a loved one who passed away this year and the knowledge that we will never experience Christmas in the same way again, the disappointment of our chronic sin that some day we seem so powerful to overcome and other days so weak to do so, or memories of sins and mistakes and failures that we regret so much and can't imagine ever forgiving ourselves for, or the time upon time when we have fallen off the wagon and wonder if God still has grace to forgive us one more time.

For those of us who can identify with one or more of these or similar experiences, the realities of angelic revelation and heavenly breakthroughs can seem pretty far-fetched and pretty unlikely this time of year. But folks, let me remind you of the truth. No matter your experience of sadness, regret, guilt, doubt, loneliness, anger, rage, addiction, fear and anxiety, disappointment, of distance from God or anger toward God, these things don't change the reality that Christ came for you, comes to you still, and will keep coming to you.

If you can identify with the darkness and despair and doubt and chronic sin and failure that are part of Advent and that remain part of who we are even after coming to Jesus, then the breaking through of heaven is a story for you. The more that you and I can identify with the darkness, the more we can and will appreciate and celebrate the breakthrough of the story when heaven came to earth and when the Savior came to tell us that the Father "so loved the world," the more we will love that Savior.

There is only one group for whom the good news of God's

coming is not good news—and that is those who do not believe they need it. For it is still quite possible for those who claim to know Christ to be in this group. We come to Jesus and forget that we still need the good news day after day after day. That we remain broken people. That we still struggle with sin. That some days we are overcome with sin. That we still struggle with mental illness. That our marriages are not perfect—none of them if we are honest. That our children are not perfect. That our families are not perfect. That our lives are not perfect. The beauty and perfection that we work so hard to create on the surface only cover up the brokenness and darkness within.

One of my favorite authors is Brennan Manning—an alcoholic who kept falling off the wagon and going back to the bottle despite being a committed follower of Jesus. Manning said this: "There is a beautiful transparency to honest disciples who never wear a false face and do not pretend to be anything but who they are."[21]

And he also spoke these comforting Gospel words:

> Because salvation is by grace through faith, I believe that among the countless number of people standing in front of the throne and in front of the Lamb, dressed in white robes and holding palms in their hands (see Revelation 7:9), I shall see the prostitute from the Kit-Kat Ranch in Carson City, Nevada, who tearfully told me that she could find no other employment to support her two-year-old son. I shall see the woman who had an abortion and is haunted by guilt and remorse but did the best she could faced with grueling alternatives; the businessman besieged with debt who sold his integrity in a series of desperate transactions; the insecure clergyman addicted to being liked, who never challenged his people from the pulpit

---

21   Brennan Manning, *The Ragamuffin Gospel* (Colorado: Multnomah Springs, 2008).

and longed for unconditional love; the sexually abused teen molested by his father and now selling his body on the street, who, as he falls asleep each night after his last "trick," whispers the name of the unknown God he learned about in Sunday School. "But how?" we ask. Then the voice says, "They have washed their robes and have made them white in the blood of the Lamb." There they are. There we are—the multitude who so wanted to be faithful, who at times got defeated, soiled by life, and beset by trials, wearing the bloodied garments of life's tribulations, but through it all, clung to faith. My friends, if this is not good news to you, you have never understood the gospel of grace.[22]

---

[22] *The Ragamuffin Gospel.*

PART FOUR

CLOSER TO THE LIGHT
THAN WE KNOW

CHAPTER 18

Nick and Nic—Closer to the Light Than Perhaps They Knew and Closer Perhaps Than Me or You
December 11, 2020

Several years ago, I was intrigued by a segment of NPR's show "Fresh Air" that I heard while doing some Christmas shopping. It was fascinating because it's not too often that Jesus is so openly discussed on National Public Radio. The interviewer and host, Terry Gross, was talking with English singer and song-writer Nick Lowe (who wrote "Cruel to be Kind" among other pop hits) regarding a Christmas album he had just produced. I was captivated as I continued listening for two reasons: 1) I wondered if I was being interviewed about Jesus on Fresh Air, what would I say; and 2) I think I have bought into the idea that the world has no time for Jesus.[23]

But here was self-proclaimed atheist Nick Lowe singing a song about Jesus and then discussing his views of Jesus. Nick said (about religion):

> I have a rather complicated relation to it. I have all the equipment to make me rather, you know, devout, I would almost say. I'm very interested in religion and different religions, and I know quite a lot about it. I love gospel music, and I love going to churches, but the one drawback is that I don't actu-

---

[23]   https://www.npr.org/2011/09/15/140037218/the-fresh-air-interview-nick-lowe.

67

ally believe in God. And it is quite a handicap, you know.... I'm the sort of person that can be reduced to tears in an empty church and feel like I'm the CEO of the Devil's organization in a full one....I love open churches and going into them looking around, but I'm not a churchgoer at all.

Nick Lowe's song was entitled "I was born in Bethlehem," in which he imagines what that first night must have been like for the holy family.[24] Terry Gross, the host, asked the obvious question: "It's a beautiful song, Nick. And I'm interested in hearing why—what you wanted to emphasize about Jesus as being there when a man needs a friend."

At this point, I was dying to hear how Nick would respond. I also wondered what I would say if asked that question on live radio. Nick replied:

Well, that's a very sort of deep question, actually. I—you know, as I say, I don't have the faith now. I certainly believe in Jesus—you know, that he existed and he was a very nice man. And who can disagree with a simple philosophy of treat other people like you like to be treated yourself? It's absolutely— nothing I can disagree with that. And I—how can I put this? So I use the name and the thought very, very easily as a sort of comfort—as a kind of comfort, in some way. And in that way, it's just like having a friend, I suppose. I mean, the way I'm talking, it sounds like I'm—you know, I'm about to go out and sign up for the nearest seminary, and you'll never see or hear from me again. But it's a hard thing to talk about, really, 'cause I'm not at all sure myself about it. But I've got a very, very simple sort of outlook to it. Yeah, that's all I can say, really.

---

24   https://genius.com/Nick-lowe-i-was-born-in-bethlehem-lyrics.

As I think about Nick Lowe and his song and his doubts, I can't help but think of another Nic (Nicodemus) who came to Jesus by night, having more guts than his peers to seek out this mysterious Messiah-like figure and to try to figure out who he was and what he was up to. And I think of Peter the disciple and his denial of Jesus, and of Thomas and his doubts about Jesus.

And what I begin to see is that Nick Lowe is just part of a band of saints perhaps, who are closer to the Kingdom than they may know and maybe even closer than those of us who swear up and down that we would never deny Jesus or be ashamed to be identified with him. It's easy to swear such things in church but a bit more challenging to be true to them when standing around a fire with our Lord's fate hanging in the balance. Peter's denial of Jesus (after three years of knowing and living with Jesus) was even more potent than Nick Lowe's. I wouldn't call Lowe's a denial as much as a set of questions he hasn't fully answered. Peter's words were like this when questioned about Jesus:

> "Woman, I don't know him" and "Man, I am not [one of them]" and "Man, I don't know what you are talking about."

And then I began to wonder about myself—would I have hemmed and hawed around about who Jesus is on National Public Radio or would I have said with clarity—"I believe that this man from Bethlehem is the Son of God!"

You know, it's easy to be hard on Nick and on the world outside our church walls. But the reality is, there is often not much difference between them and us. It's easy on Sunday morning to say, "Jesus is the Son of God." But at other times, you and I are likely to vacillate between Peter's first strong affirmation of Jesus and his second just as strong denial—some days boldly proclaiming, some days silently denying, and other days just trying to figure out who this One is to whom we have given our lives.

So as we celebrate in this season the reality of the Son of God—who has come to make us his brothers and sisters and to transform us into his likeness, can we do so with humility? Remembering that, like Peter, our lives do not always line up with what we say we believe about the Son of God, but at the same time and even so, we are called to bring the good news of God's Son to the world around us. And I believe that if we do the latter, we will be more faithful at the former—that is, if we are steadfast in sharing the good news of Jesus with those around us, we will find our faith in that same Jesus growing and being strengthened. But if we hunker down and hole up in these four church walls and keep this news to ourselves, we are at much greater risk of losing our bearings and forgetting that Jesus is indeed the Son of the Living God.

So let's not forget: We are being transformed—all of us. We are sons and daughters of God. We are brothers and sisters of Christ. And while this is excellent news for us, it is also great news for Nick and Nic and the world that God so loved and so loves still.

CHAPTER 19

Seekers Who Know Because They Seek and Those Who Don't Know Because They Won't

December 15, 2020

I n his gospel, in chapter 2, Matthew records,

> In the time of King Herod, after Jesus was born in Bethlehem of Judea, wise men from the East came to Jerusalem, asking, "Where is the child who has been born king of the Jews? For we observed his star at its rising, and have come to pay him homage...." When they had heard the king, they set out; and there, ahead of them, went the star that they had seen at its rising, until it stopped over the place where the child was. When they saw that the star had stopped, they were overwhelmed with joy. On entering the house, they saw the child with Mary his mother; and they knelt down and paid him homage. Then, opening their treasure chests, they offered him gifts of gold, frankincense, and myrrh. And having been warned in a dream not to return to Herod, they left for their own country by another road. (Matthew 2:1-2, 9-12)

Who were these mysterious Magi? How did they get to Bethlehem? What did they want? What was the star they followed? How did they know about the birth of a king of the Jews? Some suggest they were philosophers, astrologers, or astronomers from Babylon—perhaps scholars who were familiar with Israel's God because of the presence of the Hebrew Scriptures in Babylon during the Jewish exile there.

But nearly as mysterious as who these Magi are is the fact that Luke devotes so much time, as he did with the shepherds, describing their arrival to see Jesus the Christ child. And while of a much higher social standing than the shepherds, these Magi were foreigners, immigrants who should have been stopped at the border.

But God's point is clear—who gets to hear the good news first? Those for whom it is the good news—the lowest of the low and the foreigner and immigrant. King Herod? No, he was too interested in remaining King. The Jewish leaders? No, they were too interested in their own narrative of events. The shepherds? Of course, for they had no position, power, nor much of a story to speak of. The wise men? Of course, unlike most others of the day—they were seeking truth even if they didn't know what he looked like or where to find him. But anyone seeking the truth will find the truth. Jesus said that himself.

So what's wrong with the rest of us who aren't doing so much seeking for the Christ child these days? The rest of us who don't find these to be the most incredible days of wonder and joy and hope? The rest of us who hear the shepherd's story and that of the wise men and then flip back to our favorite cable news channel—one that simply reaffirms that we are correct and already know the truth?

Sometimes I think most of us go to church to hear whether what we believe to be true is reinforced or contradicted. Rather than honestly asking whether we might be the ones who are wrong when that moment of contradiction occurs, we instead blame the preacher for getting their algorithms messed up that morning. And if that preacher sticks at it long enough, we will switch churches like we switch channels. Because we are no longer seekers but knowers. And we know better than to stick by a preacher who, God forbid, might challenge our taken-for-granted reality and who might actually have the courage to raise questions that we would rather not face. For there is such comfort in knowing that we are among those who are most right and proper.

Isn't it interesting that astrologers from enemy lands showed up to worship Christ, even while his own people later wanted nothing to do with him and Herod just wanted to kill him? Here Jesus was, surrounded by people who had been anticipating a Messiah for hundreds of years but who had no idea that he was right in front of them! Why? Because they were knowers who had given up seeking a long time ago. But if there is one thing about God—he loves to fool with the wisdom of the knowers and loves to surprise the seekers with truth and knowledge. What intrigues me about these Magi is their capacity to listen to God regardless of where they were and who they were with. It was clear that they consistently had their ear to the ground listening for truth regardless of where it was coming from, and where it was coming from may have been less their concern than that they heard it in the first place!

They may have learned it from what they observed in nature. They may have learned it from Zoroastrianism, which was the only monotheistic religion in the world besides Judaism. They may have learned it from the Hebrew Scriptures. I don't think it mattered to them the source of the truth because, as students of the truth, they knew its crystal-clear ring regardless of whether it came from the Hebrew Scriptures, the stars they were studying, or the religion of Zoroastrianism.

The truth that "all truth is God's truth" has served me well, but it has not always taken me to safe places. It has served me well in that it has led me to the Christ child, but not everyone has appreciated how I got to the manger. And their disagreement with the path I took has sometimes led them, I suspect, to wonder if I got to the manger at all. And the fact that they don't see me on the path going back home with them perhaps only reinforces their doubts. But I pray that my ear like that of the Magi is always to the ground listening for truth because if it is, I could care less who I see on the journey with me unless it is other seekers of truth and of the Truth.

I keep thinking about Nick Lowe, that self-proclaimed atheist who penned a beautiful song entitled "I was born in Bethlehem." Nick is speaking for Jesus and the way that Jesus so consistently shows up as our friend. Even though Nick doesn't believe that Jesus is God, he still is seeking the quality of comfort that only divinity can provide, and I can't help but wonder if his connection to Jesus might just not be closer than he knows or than it is for lots of folks in the church.

You know, it's easy to be hard on Nick and on the world outside the church walls. Still, I'm not sure that Nick is any less of an honest seeker than the wise men, or if he is, he certainly seems to be on a journey in the direction of the Star. He just might need a friend like you or me, full of our own doubts and questions but who finds comfort from somewhere in the heavens—to walk with him to Bethlehem.

CHAPTER 20

More Are Saints Than We Recognize

I often show my students clips from the film "St. Vincent," starring Bill Murray as a drunk, no-good, gambling loser who is forced more or less to become the "babysitter" of Oliver, perhaps ten years old who lives next door with his single mom. While Vince teaches Oliver things that none of us would want our children to learn, Oliver begins to find safe refuge in Vince's presence. He learns that Vince has a wife with dementia who he continues to care for, that Vince was a hero in the Vietnam War, and that Vince makes sacrifices to feed Oliver and Vince's pet cat.[25]

And so, for a public presentation on saints, Oliver created a moving presentation about "St. Vincent," for Oliver as a child saw into the heart of Vince in ways that others and even Vince himself could not see. Oliver came to love Vince, and Vince to love Oliver. They saw each other as human beings, both marginalized from others and in need of the other. Here was a scoundrel within whom Oliver saw sainthood. But there are also saints within which there is "scoundrelhood."

Many of us know the story. King David of Israel uses his power to violate his neighbor Bathsheba, uses the same power to destroy her marriage to Uriah, and then succumbs to the power of hell to make sure that Uriah is killed in battle. Deeds done in deep darkness were possible only because David's heart contained such darkness. Somewhere

---

[25]   https://www.rottentomatoes.com/m/st_vincent.

in the depths of his being, despite all his psalms of worship, his call to praise, his naked dancing—the shadows of sin and death and destruction would emerge to reveal that all was not well in this king's heart.

Nor is it entirely well in any of our hearts as we begin this Lenten season. St. Augustine, the fourth-century bishop of Hippo in northern Africa, was aware of the shadows in his soul and prayed this: "O Lord, the house of my soul is narrow, enlarge it that thou mayest enter in. It is ruinous, O repair it! It displeases thy sight; I confess it, I know. But who shall cleanse it, or to whom shall I cry but unto thee? Cleanse me from my secret faults, O Lord, and spare thy servant from strange sins."[26]

Rediscovering this prayer at the beginning of this year, I committed myself to begin each day with it. This is a prayer that acknowledges a heart that has been dismantled, a heart in ruins, a soul that needs renovation. It is a prayer too often absent in the contemporary church and among 21st-century saints. If it were not so uncommon, I suspect that more would be willing to accept that indeed, the church as we know it is in a similar state of disrepair and ruin and dismantling—and in desperate need of the Spirit's renovation.

But renovation for our souls or our churches can only begin from the place of such confession of death, destruction, dismantledness, and darkness both within us as individuals and as the church. If it doesn't begin with me, I can't ever expect to hear such prayers from the church. And the fact that so often what we hear is defensiveness and protest from the church suggests that few of us are beginning our days with St. Augustine's prayer. Or with David's prayer of confession for that matter—who, when confronted by the prophet Nathan, finally acknowledged, after initial defensiveness, that his heart was in deep disrepair.

---

26   St. Augustine, *The Confessions of St. Augustine* (Oxford, Oxford University Press, 1998).

Have mercy on me, O God, according to your steadfast love; according to your abundant mercy, blot out my transgressions. Wash me thoroughly from my iniquity, and cleanse me from my sin. For I know my transgressions, and my sin is ever before me. Against you, you alone, have I sinned and done what is evil in your sight so that you are justified in your sentence and blameless when you pass judgment. Indeed, I was born guilty, a sinner when my mother conceived me. You desire truth in the inward being; therefore, teach me wisdom in my secret heart. Purge me with hyssop, and I shall be clean; wash me, and I shall be whiter than snow. Let me hear joy and gladness; let the bones that you have crushed rejoice. Hide your face from my sins, and blot out all my iniquities. Create in me a clean heart, O God, and put a new and right spirit within me. (Psalm 51:1-10)

Friends, if the resurrection is going to mean anything at all to us, it will begin with the confession that our hearts and our church contain shadows, destruction, death and that each is in deep need of repair and renovation. Otherwise, we do not need the resurrection or the One who came to redeem the darkness within both ourselves and the rather motley collection of saints who gather from time to time—broken, crooked, filled with secret faults and strange sins.

CHAPTER 21

When Missing the Mark Is Actually the Path to Sainthood, Not Hell
April 10, 2021

One of the richest gifts I am receiving these days is correspondence from listeners and readers of my podcast and blog who remind me that what I am giving voice to is a shared experience among many of us. We don't just regurgitate the old truths; we rediscover them. And we keep learning together—which, of course, is what faithful saints do.

I received a note from a reader who has given me permission to share it. This is a gem, friends:

> Last summer, our grandson, "Little B," at 18 months of age, became fixated on balls of all kinds, especially basketballs. He loved watching his dad, "Big B," shooting baskets into the hoop, way high up there. "Little B" did more than watch. He would march up to that hoop and shoot his basketball into the air, of course, only making a fraction of the height needed. But no worries. Off he went after that ball to bring it back—then carefully lining himself up in front of that hoop to shoot again and again and again. We observed that "Little B" never made a shot without first lining himself up in front of the hoop. That his ball never went through the hoop like "Big B's" did was apparently of no consequence for "Little B." The whole process seemed to be pure joy for him.

I treasure this picture. I think of my faith journey. In the past decade, my faith has unraveled till barely a thread remains to flutter in the breeze. In an NPR interview with Terry Gross, actor Kerry Washington said, "I practice acts of faith to engender faith." That seems to describe my present state. I don't know if God is there or if God cares, but I continue to line up before the hoop to shoot. My shots (acts of faith) only make it a fraction of the distance. I don't hear from God. I don't "know" things of which I was formerly convinced. Still, I continue to line up and make my shots. I know this: that I love the story of Jesus even if, in the end, it's just a story among many stories. This is a sad place for me, and I long to see a light on the path ahead.

I grew up hearing over and over again that the definition of sin was to "miss the mark" and that I was guilty of sin because when I threw the darts at the dart board I repeatedly missed, when I tried to clear the bar for the high jump I frequently fell short, that my efforts to be good enough were never good enough for a God who demanded perfection. But I wish someone had told me and all of us who were more than aware of our shortcomings that this was not a definition of sin but the Law. Paul makes it clear that the Law was created to remind us that we couldn't keep it. And the problem with living by the Law is that we are in a state of continual guilt, shame, and awareness of our failure.

Yes, the church told me that the good news was that Jesus came to deliver me from my sins and failures, but I never knew what to do with the fact that my sins and failures continued and that since I hadn't reached perfection with Jesus, I must still be living in sin. And so I spent my life trying to be better, jump higher, throw more accurately—somehow proving to myself and those around me that I finally had achieved Jesus and overcome sin.

In other words, the church so many of us have been given is not a church of grace but one of the Law. We are Old Testament churches that teach about Jesus but don't receive Jesus, that teach grace but live by the law. And as I listen to so many of my listeners and readers of my blog and podcast, I am beginning to understand how many have left the church because its preaching never lived up to its promise. And some days, I feel full of grief and anger because of the lies of hell we've propagated and the truths of heaven we've hidden.

Here are just a few stories I've heard: An individual who left the church because it taught that mental illness was sin—and this individual's family had a long history of depression and suicide. An older saint who has lived all of their life under a burden of never being adequate only to recently tell me, with tears, that upon sharing with their father of his conversion, the father, a professing Christian and church goer responded, "Well, now you are really going to need to be good." And a church that recently asked me to speak but in their description of the event noted that if we "do church right, then...." Folks, I'm tired of this kind of teaching— teaching that denies our humanity, that holds a bar over our heads that God himself knows we can't achieve, and a belief that we can ever do church right, and that if we do, so God will bless us.

This weekend a pastor who works with sex offenders emailed me and told me that he met with a group of these men as he regularly does, and he suggested they take communion. One man refused, saying that he was too far from God. Then the pastor shared my podcast from several days ago about shame, and when he was done, the man said, "Okay, I will take communion now, and I am ready to try to walk with Jesus once again."

In my reading last week, I came upon a more accurate definition of sin that is truly good news. It comes from the mystic Simone Weil. In it, she describes that Jesus went the furthest possible distance from God on the cross, a greater distance than any of us can ever go—separated from the Father because he was accursed as the Scripture declares. And Weil says this: "[Those] struck down by affliction are at the foot of the cross, almost at the greatest possible distance from God. It must not be thought that sin is a greater distance. Sin is not a distance, it is a turning of our gaze in the wrong direction."[27]

Friends, we can never hit the mark of the law, but we can always turn our gaze back to Jesus. And when we do we will always find him smiling at us, never rebuking us because we missed that damn mark again, never criticizing us for failing to jump high enough, but always saying, "Come back into my safe and loving arms, for today and for every day hereafter, you shall be with me in paradise."

And that my friends, is the truth of the Resurrection that I choose to live within!

---

27   Simone Weil, *Love in the Void: Where God Finds Us.* (Walden, NY: Plough).

PART FIVE

A GOD IN THE DARK?

CHAPTER 22

Do the Heavens Hear?
Do the Heavens Care?
March 5, 2021

I remember well the night when I ran screaming up College Avenue thirteen years ago, raging at a God who seemed so unfair, angry at One who seemed more like darkness than light, so furious with a God who seemed not to care about the diagnosis of ovarian cancer that Heidi had received. Some days and nights, there are no answers from heaven.

Last night Heidi and I watched a film about Ma Rainey, the "mother" of blues in the 1920s. Ma's story was a dark one. An African-American woman, gifted by her Creator with a remarkable voice, she was desirable to white folks in the music industry but only because of that voice and the profits it made them.[28]

Her band of itinerant musicians also knew darkness, having been traumatized, victimized, and dehumanized by centuries of slavery and Jim Crow. At one point, one of them curses God for the memories of a mother, gang-raped when he was eight years old. Looking to the heavens, he seethed with bitterness, hatred, anger, and despair. And as hard as it was to hear and watch, I can't help but wonder if that cursing and those tears were a prayer that is better prayed than not. And certainly, if we believe in a loving God, this is certainly a prayer that such a deity can well handle.

---

[28]   https://g.co/kgs/LXa2du.

If we are human and willing to be honest and to abandon just for a moment our self-righteousness, which of us hasn't looked to the heavens with anger, fear, doubt, and a sense of deep abandonment?

The Psalmist certainly did:

> As a deer longs for flowing streams, so my soul longs for you, O God. My soul thirsts for God, for the living God. When shall I come and behold the face of God? My tears have been my food day and night, while people say to me continually, "Where is your God?" These things I remember, as I pour out my soul: how I went with the throng, and led them in procession to the house of God, with glad shouts and songs of thanksgiving, a multitude keeping festival. Why are you cast down, O my soul, and why are you disquieted within me? (Psalm 42:1-5)

This is the Psalm that I have been hanging out in this week, and yes, I did not include in the passage the reminders and affirmations of God that the Psalmist eventually gets to in his prayer. It is essential to sit with the sense of rejection, pain, sorrow, and abandonment that the Psalmist feels before we jump to the promises that God has made, before we put on a mask that denies the current pain. Who knows the length of time it took before the Psalmist could get up the courage to repeat to himself those words of hope and trust and confidence that would eventually come? Perhaps it was weeks or months or years or a lifetime.

Jumping too quickly to the affirmations of hope, trust, and confidence in God, whether said to ourselves or others, can sometimes interfere with the Spirit's work. Such work can be done in us only when we are standing at the edge of the abyss looking into nothingness or running up the street screaming at the heavens for injustice or even cursing the heavens for the seeming absence of God in a moment of trauma. For in these moments, no affirmation of hope or trust, or confidence is usually heard.

St. Paul himself reminds us that all of creation itself screams, moans, groans, and decays. And even "we ourselves, who have the first fruits of the Spirit, groan inwardly as we wait eagerly for...the redemption of our bodies." Even we.

Many of us in my community are aware of a young man's tragic and sudden illness with so much promise, now suffering from an aggressive brain tumor. I ran into a friend at Costco this week, and as we talked about this young man and his family, we stopped in the refrigerator section and prayed for him, for his family, and for God's mercy.

For in the injustice and unfairness and unanswerable questions, where else can we turn? Except to the One who in our pain of feeling his abandonment groans also says St. Paul, groans with us in ways that earthly "words cannot express." God groans. God feels pain. God experiences injustice. And I have often said, God weeps with us.

After and perhaps even during the screaming and maybe even the cursing with the Psalmist, we whisper to ourselves and those around us, "Hope thou in God: for I shall yet praise him for the help of his countenance."

CHAPTER 23

God With PTSD?
March 28, 2021

I've been thinking a lot about the trauma that Jesus experienced during Holy Week. I've heard folks describe the physical suffering of Christ in great detail. But rarely do we hear about the emotional, mental, and spiritual trauma that most certainly had to accompany the beatings, mocking, cross-carrying, crown-of-thorns wearing, and abandonment by his last remaining hope—a Father in heaven who turned away.

I suspect, in part, this failure is due to our difficulty in acknowledging or understanding, or knowing what to do with our own and others' trauma. As a result, we tend to deny it, bury it, or even laugh it off. But inevitably, its impact on our lives will take a toll and result in more significant trauma for us and those we love.

In a challenging time in my life, it was the image of Jesus on the cross, arms outstretched, and absorbing the deep pain I was experiencing that enabled me to go on. It was the God of the crucifix, the God on the cross, that gave me hope. In a new way, I recognized that Christ had come not just to forgive me for the ways that I had tried to make it on my own, but that he had also come to carry my pain, to absorb my pain into his heart, and to release me from the need for revenge by giving my pain to him.

Now imagine Christ having done that for all of humanity—in that one moment in history both to carry the pain of all history— past, present, and future- and forgive the perpetrators of that pain.

To have carried and absorbed all of the injustice, the abuse, the violence, the pain of a world that had rejected wholeness and life and light. While his doing so did not remove the impact of trauma on us, it also had to impact God. For God was traumatized like never before. God experienced emotional, spiritual, and mental anguish like never before. And I believe that God was never the same afterward.

Just as Christ carried to heaven the scars in his hand and side, I cannot help but believe that he also carried and continues to do so—the emotional and mental trauma experienced and absorbed that week. In some way, I wonder, does God have PTSD?

I don't think this question is a heretical one, given what the author of Hebrews says about Jesus:

> Now that we know what we have—Jesus, this great High Priest with ready access to God—let's not let it slip through our fingers. We don't have a priest who is out of touch with our reality. He's been through weakness and testing, experienced it all—all but the sin. So let's walk right up to him and get what he is so ready to give. Take the mercy, accept the help. (Hebrews 4:14-16, *The Message*)

This means that Jesus identifies with every experience of pain and difficulty and suffering—not just sees but also empathizes with—is reminded of his own. I have said for a long time that I believe God grieves with us. Because things were not to be this way. And because Jesus identifies with us in the trauma of our lives, it also means that he knows precisely how to pray for us. No one else may understand. No one else may know how to pray for us. But Jesus gets it fully.

And for this reason, I repeatedly remind folks that "God always provides a pathway" through the uncertainties and difficulties we experience and that he cares more about us finding that pathway than we do. St. Paul said it this way:

> "No test or temptation that comes your way is beyond the
> course of what others have had to face. All you need to remem-
> ber is that God will never let you down; he'll never let you be
> pushed past your limit; he'll always be there to help you come
> through it." (I Corinthians 10:13, *The Message*)

One of those others was God himself—the Word became
flesh.

CHAPTER 24

Mary, Lazarus, and Jesus: Deranged, Deviant, or Divine?

March 20, 2021

I'm reading John 12 this morning. You know, it's the story of Mary, Martha, and their brother Lazarus once again—a trio of siblings with whom Jesus has come to feel safe and with whom he is restored and renewed. They are the kind of folks that, no matter what others in the church say about you, have come to trust you, believe you, and simultaneously find restoration while with you. They are Psalm 23 kind of folks. They know how to set a table for you in the presence of your enemies.

Perhaps this trio of siblings knew just how to do this because Jesus himself had already done this for them—validated them with his company, legitimated their value, and by his very presence had become a safe place to hang out from their enemies. For enemies and resistance they certainly had—in fact, it would appear that the closer they came to Jesus and the longer they spent time with him and the more they came to life in his presence, the greater the multitude who opposed them.

The already righteous and healthy have a way of doing that—resisting those who suddenly find new intimacy with Jesus, suddenly discover new revelations from Jesus, suddenly understand that Jesus is worth wasting one's most significant possessions upon. And they have the vocabulary to describe what they believe they see in such folks—mentally ill, ungrounded, gone off the deep end, heretical, deceived, and more. All language is valuable not because it expresses reality but because it brings comfort to those who embrace it—and the satisfaction of knowing that we are not like "them."

Sociologists are slow to label people as mentally ill. Why? Because we recognize that such folks might just be seeing a reality that somehow is being missed by the rest of us, that perhaps their perspectives are simply deviant and not deranged. If we can objectify those who are different from us with labels that soothe us, then we can get about the business of our day without worrying about them anymore.

And so Judas, one of the twelve but a thief at heart, responds to Mary's deep expression of love, criticizes her for having her priorities all screwed up. "It's about the poor," he said, unaware of indeed just how poor his own soul was. But Jesus pushed back, "Leave her alone," setting a boundary around this friend whom he loved and who had just made abundantly clear her love for him.

But the drama wasn't over yet. A crowd began to gather—folks who wanted to see Lazarus—risen from the dead, the stench of death long gone, now walking around more full of life than ever and more full of life than most of them. But while some came to gawk, others came to murder—not just Lazarus, but the very movement of the Divine that had brought Lazarus back from the dead in the first place.

The resurrection of Lazarus was a reminder to these leaders that the power they clung to was nothing compared to that of this prophet and mystic from Nazareth, this wandering sage. Many of those who were lost—including so many in the very churches of these leaders—"were going over to and putting their faith in [Jesus]."

I suspect that what drove these leaders nuts was less about Jesus and Mary and Lazarus and more about themselves and the loss of power, prestige, and privilege that lay ahead if they allowed this man from Galilee to carry on his little circus among the misfits much longer.

The reaction of the enemy of all goodness and the Good himself is predictable—steal, kill, and destroy all that is life and that flows from that Life. But the good news for Mary, Martha, Lazarus, and for all of us is that the One who prepares a table for us in front of our enemies will also keep overflowing our cups with oil, enough to ensure that "goodness and love will follow us all the days of our lives."

And someday, our enemies and the enemy of us all will return to their homes while we go on to "dwell in the house of the Lord forever" and forever and forever and forever. Amen.

CHAPTER 25

"Sometimes I Think God Is Powerless to Stop the Suffering." "That's Bad Theology," He Replied

December 23, 2020

In 2000 I was diagnosed with papillary thyroid cancer and underwent two surgeries and three years of treatment. I was thirty-five years old. In that same year, I was ordained as Lead Pastor of our Mennonite congregation in Elizabethtown, PA. And at the end of that year, as Advent began, a letter was circulated calling for my resignation.

I turned to a Christian therapist for help. In one of our sessions, I mused: "I sometimes think that God is powerless to intervene in our suffering." And I think I may have added that I believe he weeps along with us. If I didn't add that, it has become something that I sincerely believe now. My therapist bristled at this comment: "That's bad theology, don't you think?"

That response is one of the things that bothers me most about a theology that refuses to look God in the face and say, "Where in the world are you this Christmas season? Why are you allowing this to happen to me?" For such a theology is not what I need, nor am I sure that what I really need is theology at all. What I need is someone to be present with me when I am suffering. Christian faith that reduces God to theology has become a thing of the head, not the heart, a thing abstract and not of the human soul, inert to pain and suffering

94

rather than one that recognizes that pain and suffering are our lot this side of the new heaven and new earth.

Nor is such a theology reflected in the Scripture. Each week I hang out in the morning in a particular Psalm, and last week it was in the seventy-seventh chapter where we hear this lament: "Will the Lord reject forever? Will he never show his favor again? Has his unfailing love vanished forever? Has his promise failed for all time? Has God forgotten to be merciful? Has he in anger withheld his compassion?" (NIV)

While the Psalmist will eventually round the bend and begin to reflect on the mercy and goodness of God that they experienced in the past, we don't know that this shift took place in a day, a week, a month, or even after several years of lament. I love the Scripture because it is honest—raw with pain, raw about our brokenness, raw in the questions it screams at the Almighty! Why God? Why this year? Why now? Why did you take her? Why this diagnosis? Why the loss of 300,000 Americans and many more around the world in this year of Covid-19? Why the break-up of my marriage? Why the loss of our child in miscarriage? Why is my son still in prison—hasn't he served enough time? Will you never show us favor again? Have you forgotten your love? Has your promise failed for all time? Why are you so angry with us?

The Gospel of Matthew records that King Herod, upon hearing from the Wise Men that Jesus had been born and that he had come from heaven as a King, then decreed that all little boys of a certain age were to be destroyed to make sure he wiped out whoever this new child king was. And Matthew says this tragedy was a fulfillment of an old prophetic word that "a voice is heard in Ramah, weeping and great mourning. Rachel weeping for her children and refusing to be comforted because they are no more."

Refusing to be comforted—for Rachel, who lost her little

one because of Christmas, no theology could bring her peace. For Rachel, who lost her mother or father to Covid-19, there is no comfort this year. There is no comfort for the single mom who lost her job and, as of this morning, still doesn't know if her unemployment benefits will continue in 2021. There is no comfort for the African-American or Latinx extended family who lost more than one relative to Covid-19. So don't tell me and don't tell them that God is so powerful as to change all of this, because if that is the case, he is the cruelest deity one can imagine. As C. S. Lewis observes—my paraphrase—God created a world in which he cannot just freely, willy-nilly intervene without violating the very laws he builds into the creation, laws of order, consequence, and human freedom.

So don't tell me that God is not weeping this morning for all of the pain, loss, and political paralysis and polarization of this year that has no guarantee of abating in 2021. And don't tell me he hasn't had some second thoughts about how he set this all up. I don't know, but don't give me easy answers—they are not what I need.

Indeed, if it were answers we needed, God would have created another set of stone tablets and displayed them in the temple. If it was theology we needed, God could have made a seminary to give us answers to our questions. If it was more knowledge that we needed, God could have started a university.

But no, what God knew we needed more than anything else was hope that this is not all that there is, a promise that a new heaven and earth are coming, and the empathy of One who would come to know what it was like to be human because he would become one of us. What God knew we needed most was his presence and the presence of a child who would, through his own suffering and death, take upon him the brokenness of the world, the pain of the world, the curses of the world to change the direction of that world from one with its compass needle pointed toward hell to one with that needle pointed toward the new heaven and new earth.

When Heidi and I separated in 1990, it was the most painful time in my life. It was also a time when I finally acknowledged that I was a broken human being. I lived in a religious culture that hid sin and brokenness in the silence of a theology that refused to recognize the shadows and demons with which I wrestled. Our broken marriage broke the silence around the mental illness I had lived with, tormented by OCD since a kid. It revealed to the world around me that I was not all that I appeared to be.

And in those days of brokenness, I also found freedom, and I found peace, and I found God like it was for the first time. Any society that keeps our brokenness undercover is a society that also keeps the wondrous truth of Christ's coming undercover as well. For it is only in acknowledging the reality of our shadows and brokenness and beat-upness that we have any interest in reaching out for the One Answer.

CHAPTER 26

When Christmas Disappoints
December 26. 2020

Christmas is bound to disappoint. The anticipation of the day—the gifts, time with family, the food, the unique rituals that families create over the generations—sets us up for disappointment. Like so many things in life, it is the height of the anticipation that sets the stage for the descent into reality. The reality of a family conflict on Christmas morning. The fact that after receiving a medical diagnosis, this just might be the last Christmas morning with one's children. The reality of gifts that were not appreciated by those we gave them to. The truth that someone we loved is no longer with us this Christmas. The reality that our marriage is broken, and we have to let our kids know we are splitting up. The fact of uncertainty in a pandemic that has brought division, poverty, unemployment, despair, and a landscape stripped of the familiar. The reality of a gift we had looked forward to receiving. But it arrived broken and could not be replaced—and on and on.

It is easy to blame the thing that went wrong: the impatient and angry parent, the crying child, the half-baked ham, the broken new toy, or even the medical diagnosis that leaves us in limbo. But what if the most profound disappointment is not related to a thing or even a situation as much as to how God has created us.

We were not created for pain. We were not designed for disappointment. We were created for the Garden of Eden, a place of beauty, of unity with one another, a place overflowing with the love and goodness of God, a place where death had not yet visited, a site where work was always a joy, an area of the greatest safety and security. And so here we are in this place where what we were created for is not where we have ended up. Of course, we will be disappointed.

Perhaps that is why we are always anticipating and always looking forward—looking to what is next, expecting the best, trying to recreate what we had in Eden initially. Created for the best, we keep looking forward to finding it.

Our grandson Ezra is at the stage of toddlerhood where he is always looking forward to the subsequent discovery: "This?" he constantly asks. And when you tell him that it is a book or a bird or a firetruck or a train or a dog, he quickly moves on to the next thing. "This?" he repeats. For a while, his focus was on our dog Buffy, but for the most part, he has now moved on to the birds or Pappy's model trains or whatever Grammy happens to be doing in the kitchen. He is constantly discovering, always looking forward.

Or perhaps we were born to anticipate the best, born to look forward to what is next, born to discover. And those qualities of human freedom built into our humanity by God served us well in the safe place of the Garden. But those qualities also led us to that one apple tree that was off-limits to us. They are the qualities that continue motivating us to move on to the next thing in a world where only One can satisfy. Only one decision resolves our restlessness—and that One is he who created this anticipation within us in the first place—expectation for God himself—to know him, love him, be present to him, be accepted by him, be known by him, and on and on.

Like our first parents, we are sure there must be a catch—somewhere somehow there is something better than God, something more appealing, something more attractive. But this is only because we have not dwelt with God in the way he came to live with us. Because we have not searched him out in the same way that he searches us out.

It is also true that the most meaningful experiences are those that we are least prepared to experience or that we never anticipated. Then, once having them, we try all our lives to recreate them, like the addict that keeps coming back for the first high that they can never recapture. It's not that the experience was so much better the first time around but that we had invested so little in its anticipation and preparation. It took our breath away because we had so little to do with it, and the more we try to recreate something, the more likely we are to be disappointed in what we've created.

These days there are few things more special than Ezra running toward Heidi and me with his arms wide open and a big smile on his face that tells us we are loved just because we are Pappy and Grammy and that Ezra is loved just because he is Ezra. I keep thinking that the image of Ezra running to us is precisely that image of God running to us with his arms wide open, grinning from ear to ear. It's not because we've done it all right or well or perfectly, and it's not because we've done it all. But it is because we belong to him, were made by him, were made with his imprint upon us, were made as reflections of God himself. But until we understand this, we will keep anticipating and keep being disappointed.

As a pastor couple who has prepared dozens of couples for their wedding day and been with them on that day, we know there is perhaps no other day when the stakes seem to be higher in terms of perfection—the things that could go wrong are a multitude. And so, to ensure against anything less than perfection, we even practice with the couple getting married. But invariably, something goes amiss. Buy for the couple whose eyes are on each other and their life together, the amiss matters little, if at all. In the same way, for those of us who know God's infinite love and with whom we have developed a life, what Paul says in II Corinthians 4 rings true. These momentary trials are nothing compared to the coming glory, whether the problems and disappointments are on Christmas Day or any other day of the year for that matter.

CHAPTER 27

No Fear of the Fowler's Snare
January 12, 2021

It was time to take down our Christmas tree once again. I was particularly sad this year, with the memories of our little grandson Ezra hunkered down with Pappy by the train controls, learning to make the whistle blow and grinning from ear to ear. But while the tree had to go, the memories would remain. And so will the train, which I've decided this year to make a permanent thing in our basement, so Pappy and Ezra can continue to make memories all year round.

In setting up our tree, I had been especially mindful about stringing the Christmas lights into the middle of the tree, even wiring them to the branches, and using more lights than ever before. I would, and I did, fill this tree with lights. Doing so seemed appropriate for how dark it had been this year.

We enjoyed that tree for weeks, but then the time came to part with it. So that I wouldn't get tree needles all over the floor while taking off the tangle and mess of lights that I now realized I had created, I took the tree in its base to the dark front porch, where only our dim lamp provided a bit of light, but a very bit. As I struggled to get the lights off, I thought I glimpsed something in the tree. A nest? Surely not! I couldn't have missed a nest in all of the stringing of those lights that I had done. But I looked again, and sure enough—a tiny, very tiny nest of tightly woven grass tucked against the trunk of the tree, and with a few pine needles on the bottom as if to provide for the little ones a softer resting place. I pried the nest off the trunk, but it didn't come easily. The mother bird had tied it into the tree so that no amount of wind or storm could harm her little ones. If the nest was going anywhere, the tree would have to go along.

When I showed Heidi the nest, her first response was, "You didn't see it in the light but only in the dark." Curiously, when all was bright, I had missed that nest. In all of my efforts to create, I hadn't seen what was already created. Only in the dark as I dismantled that tree at the end of the season would I discover the nest.

And I was reminded of Psalm 91:

> Whoever dwells in the shelter of the Most High will rest in the shadow of the Almighty. I will say of the Lord, "He is my refuge and my fortress, my God, in whom I trust." Surely he will save you from the fowler's snare and from the deadly pestilence. He will cover you with his feathers, and under his wings, you will find refuge; his faithfulness will be your shield and rampart. You will not fear the terror of night, nor the arrow that flies by day, nor the pestilence that stalks in the darkness, nor the plague that destroys at midday. A thousand may fall at your side, ten thousand at your right hand, but it will not come near you. You will only observe with your eyes and see the punishment of the wicked. If you say, "The Lord is my refuge," and you make the Most High your dwelling, no harm will overtake you, no disaster will come near your tent. For he will command his angels concerning you to guard you in all your ways; they will lift you up in their hands so that you will not strike your foot against a stone. You will tread on the lion and the cobra; you will trample the great lion and the serpent. "Because she loves me," says the Lord, "I will rescue her; I will protect her, for she acknowledges my name. She will call on me, and I will answer her; I will be with her in trouble, I will

deliver her and honor her. With long life I will satisfy her and show her my salvation." (Excerpts from Psalm 91, NIV with Kanagy pronoun edits)

This was the Psalm that gave Heidi comfort night after night in the wake of her diagnosis of ovarian cancer in 2008. And like all timeless truth and Truth himself, it always remains a comfort. We have learned over the years that the darkness never entirely goes away and often lies in the shadows awaiting what it assumes is the right time to bare its teeth and roar back, reminding us of its presence.

The Psalmist knew this. He understood that while there was One under whose feathers and wings he was protected, there was still a "fowler" out there somewhere seeking to snare both the Psalmist and the One under whose wings the Psalmist dwelt. But the writer also knew that there wasn't a chance that the fowler could ever snare the One under whom he found refuge, and so there was no chance that the fowler could ever really touch the Psalmist either.

Oh, the darkness threatens. Heidi and I know that well. But its threats are pretty predictable, and even the timing of those threats is relatively predictable as well. The tools of the fowler of darkness are the same time and again—fear, threats, intimidation, and shadows. But these tools are also limited by the One whose presence becomes the shadow under which we find safety. Isn't this an interesting twist? We are pictured as being under the wings of the Great Dove, and the enemy is portrayed as the hunter out to get us. But his real target is not us, but the One under whose wings we dwell. And folks, that One has already refused to be trapped, for he already escaped the threat of the trap, and stormed the doors of that trap to rescue those caught within it. The reality is that the trap remains just a threat to those of us who rest with the everlasting arms beneath us.

I have long loved this word from Quaker writer George Fox:

And Friends, though you may have tasted of the power and been convinced and have felt the light, yet afterward you may feel winter storms, tempests, and hail, and be frozen, in frost and cold and a wilderness and temptations. Be patient and still in the power and still in the light that doth convince you, to keep your minds to God; in that be quiet, that you may come to the summer, that your flight be not in the winter. For if you sit still in the patience which overcomes in the power of God, there will be no flying; for the husbandman, after he has sown his seed, his is patient. For by the power and by the light you will come to see through and feel over winter storms, tempests, and all the coldness, barrenness, emptiness. And the same light and power will go over the tempter's head, which power and light were before he was. And so in the light standing still you will see your salvation, you will see the Lord's strength, you will feel the small rain, you will feel the fresh springs in the power and light, your minds being kept low; for that which is out of the power and the light lifts up. But in the power and light you will see God revealing his secrets, inspiring, and his gifts coming to you, through which your hearts will be filled with God's love; praise to him that lives forever more, in which light and power his blessings are received. And so the eternal power of the Lord Jesus Christ preserve and keep you in that. And so live everyone in the power of God that you may all come to be heirs of that and know that to be your portion, and the kingdom that hath no end, and an endless life, which the seed is heir of. And so feel that overall set, which hath the promise and blessing of God.[29]

And so we can always shout to the shadows with the saints, "Where, O death is your victory? Where O death is your sting?"

---

[29]   George Fox, *Journal of George Fox* (Cambridge: University Press, 1911), 224.

PART SIX

DENYING THE DARKNESS,
AND SOMETIMES THE LIGHT

CHAPTER 28

There Is No Light Without Entering the Darkness
March 17, 2021

This week I talked to students in my criminology course about leadership; leaders always bring change, and they always lose something in the process, usually something of themselves. I reminded them that if they, as graduates, entered the current Criminal Justice system, despite all of the calls for change that folks are making these days, any efforts to bring about that change would be met with resistance and sabotage. True transformation never comes to an organization or a group without the leader taking hits from the very people who were so excited about the promise of change when she/he was first called to lead.

Anyone who enters a space where change is called for and needed must know that they will lose something of themselves in the process. If they do not, they have not led through change but merely moved some chairs around. Any leader who looks to their people for affirmation as the measure of whether or not they are making a difference is not really committed to transformation. Genuine and authentic change-makers usually hear little back from those who are experiencing that change. Oh, they might receive affirmation on the day of their death, but few change agents will hear it during their lifetime. And any leader who anticipates close friendships with those they are leading is destined just to reinforce the status quo. Indeed what passes for friendship is sometimes just an effort to neutralize the leader's punch. Flattery, too, has the same effect.

In one of my podcast episodes, I interviewed Kevin Ressler, Black American and advocate for social and racial justice. Kevin addressed the complicity of the white church in the ongoing systemic racism within the U.S. Kevin's passion and words rung and stung with truth. Unusually so. His statements were sharp and cut through the fog of ambiguity like only those who have indeed counted the cost can do.[30] So I wasn't at all surprised when Kevin reflected on the fact that he has lived since high school with a sense of the possibility that he might not live beyond the age of forty. His two favorite authors, Stephen Crane and Edgar Allen Poe died at about this age.

Over the last year, a repeated theme of mine has been the necessity of living with the day of our death in mind, with the horizon and the sunset in full view ahead of us. Without a resignation to the day of our death, we will always hedge our bets; we will never fully speak the truth; we will always withdraw from a full-frontal attack on the darkness. But those who have come to grips with their future death, who have given themselves up before that time comes, have nothing to lose and everything to gain by entering the darkness. And as they do so, they soon learn the rewards—for there are so few others doing the same.

Attorney Bryan Stephenson tells the story of when he met with Rosa Parks and her friend as a young activist for racial justice—both involved in the Montgomery bus boycott. As Bryan described his work and what he hoped to accomplish on behalf of those wrongfully accused and incarcerated, Rosa Parks' friend looked at him and said, "Son, you are going to have to be brave, brave, brave."[31]

Brave, brave, brave is what characterized Kevin Ressler's words

30   https://youtu.be/TTEJIO2d7Jg.
31   https://g.co/kgs/AsQKUQ.

this week. And brave, brave, brave is what characterized Christian activists before him.

For a community whose Lord told us that life only comes from death and that following him will require us to be brave, brave, brave, we who are part of the dominant culture church show remarkably little bravery these days, let alone change and transformation. For a year, I have argued that the Covid-19 pandemic was just the kind of season for such change. While I often have felt my perspective unheeded, maybe God is bringing that change regardless of our response to this season. As another one of my guests, long-time missionary Jewel Showalter said recently: "Perhaps this season of history is God's way of pruning a nominal church." Amen Jewel. Amen.

CHAPTER 29

I'd Rather Have Jesus—Even in the Shadows or as a Mirage
February 19, 2021

I'd rather have Jesus than silver or gold; I'd rather be His than have riches untold...[32]

I've been listening to this song by Jim Reeves for the past few weeks in the mornings as I sit with the Lord. It reminds me of what author Anne Lamont says unapologetically—that she is "Jesusy." When push comes to shove, I now care less about what others think, whether I'm meeting their expectations or conforming to the church's taken-for-granted realities. I want to know that I am becoming more authentically who Jesus created and calls me to be.

After a year of rage and tears following my diagnosis of Parkinson's disease, I told our congregation that I had experienced a new conversion to Jesus.[33] But this time because I had experienced his love like never before. I can't explain why for sure, but what I do know is that in my grief and in my pain of that initial year of my diagnosis, Jesus came to me as I had never experienced him coming to me before.

With God hidden in the shadows of my religious ruminations for decades, my time with God in the morning was more like hell many days than anything akin to heaven—repeatedly praying for

---

32   https://www.google.com/search?q=i+d+rather+have+jesus+lyrics.

33   https://youtu.be/tAWva6cPSIc.

forgiveness of sins that were never sins in the first place, confessing over and over again things he had long ago forgotten. But in the shadows, he remained, and on some of my better days, I would catch a glimpse of his smile, enough to carry me through the next few weeks of tortured guilt and shame. I pastored this way, taught this way, wrote this way, and lived much of my life this way.

Faced with Parkinson's disease four years ago, I began to give myself a break. And why not—I began in a deeper way than ever to accept that I was weak, fragile, mortal, and my life such a fleeting thing. And in the days I have left, I want to grab all of the joy that I can, the peace that I can, and the love that I can. And while those things were so foreign to me most days, I had seen just enough of that smile to know that he had not gone anywhere and that he was waiting for me to understand that I am loved "just as I am, without one plea."

Suddenly a song that had sent me walking night after night to the altar at the Brunk Revivals in my hometown of Belleville, Pennsylvania—less because I needed saving and more because the church didn't know how to assure a guilt-ridden kid that the words of that song were actually about God's love and not God's condemnation—finally began to speak to my heart. Hearing those lyrics anew, I have listened to that old hymn over and over again.

I don't know. I could be all wrong. Maybe Jesus is a mirage. Maybe it was nothing except my imagination that I saw in those shadows for so many years. A Facebook friend recently challenged me, noting: "The fact is (in my mind) that we know nothing about God, and we need to get very comfortable with that reality. I'm really hoping the younger generations discover and embrace that innate goodness we carry and act on that engenderment and not be consumed by the need to know and define its source because we lose authenticity the second we begin claiming we know things that we simply, in our humanness, have no way of knowing."

I responded: "Thank you for sharing your reflections. As I tell my students when I share my faith journey, "This is my theological perspective and my experience with God, but I do not put that on you. This is my story, and this is my song, but I will not demand that it be yours. That is enough for me, and in that, I am living with a sense of peace, rest, and contentment that I never had before. I now wake each morning knowing that he waits for me, just glad that I showed up again. That I don't have to spend half an hour confessing my sins repeatedly to one who took care of them a couple thousand years ago. That I am deeply loved each morning 'just as I am.'"

And I think again of those disciples on the road to Emmaus, unable to see or comprehend the One who walked with them, the One who chose to stay in the shadows until they broke bread together. Then he revealed himself, and I suspect it was with a smile. Then he was gone again. But that smile, if they were anything like me, was enough to keep them walking toward the new heaven and new earth.

CHAPTER 30

Those Who Refuse the Bread Are so Easy to Spot
April 4, 2021

I've been listening in the morning to the hymn "Abide with me." This song was written during the Civil War by Martin Lowrie Hofford—a period in U.S. history that many suggest as a parallel to the division and polarization of our current context. The first verse goes like this: "Abide with me, fast falls the eventide. The darkness deepens, Lord, with me abide. When other helpers fail, and comforts flee. Help of the helpless, oh, abide with me."

Perhaps the central theme of my preaching over the past decade has been just this: "Nurture your life with God. Come to know him. Come to know his deep love for you. Just as we need to eat and drink, so we need to feed upon the One who is the Bread of Life." I have repeatedly said that if we do not develop a life with God, we will have no foundation to stand upon when trouble comes. There is only so much that others can do for us in such moments—and "when other helpers fail, and comforts flee," we are left with the reality of just how thin our life with God has been.

In John 6, Jesus tells those around him that he is the bread that comes down from God:

> I am the bread of life. Whoever comes to me will never go hungry, and whoever believes in me will never be thirsty. But as I told you, you have seen me and still you do not believe. All

those the Father gives me will come to me, and whoever comes to me I will never drive away. For I have come down from heaven not to do my will but to do the will of him who sent me. And this is the will of him who sent me, that I shall lose none of all those he has given me, but raise them up at the last day. For my Father's will is that everyone who looks to the Son and believes in him shall have eternal life, and I will raise them up at the last day. (NIV)

Predictably, those around Jesus again began to grumble at his words, reminding each other that he was no one other than Joseph and Mary's son. So it was highly improbable that he could really be bread from heaven.

As I transition out of ministry, one of my greatest griefs is the recognition that while some have heard and responded, evidenced by the peace they express and the stillness one sees in their lives, it is also clear that others have not done so. How can one tell those who have regularly eaten of the Bread of Life from those who have not? The same way that Jesus could tell—the grumbling gives it away.

It's hard to be a chronic grumbler when you are abiding with Christ. It's challenging to remain bitter and angry when your hands are open to receive the bread from heaven. But grumblers inevitably close their hands in a fist, and closed hands have a hard time accepting anything, let alone the Bread of Life.

A steady diet of that Bread brings healing, touches us where we most need to be touched, resolves the answers that others cannot give us, and meets the deep hunger in our souls. And then it is from this place of fulfillment and nourishment that we greet the world and that we greet one another.

And whether we greet the world grumbling or greet the world with grace has everything to do with whether we have practiced abiding with the only One who can satisfy our weary souls.

As our congregation regathers, I will be listening for the grumbling—it will tell me and everyone else who spent this past year abiding and who did not, who spent this last year of isolation feeding on the Bread from heaven and who did not.

And I will keep preaching the same word.

CHAPTER 31

Can We Talk Ourselves to Sleep?
May 29, 2021

O Lord, my heart is not lifted up, my eyes are not raised too high; I do not occupy myself with things too great and too marvelous for me. But I have calmed and quieted my soul, like a child quieted at its mother's breast; like a child that is quieted is my soul. O Israel, hope in the Lord from this time forth and forevermore. (Psalm 131, NIV)

David writes this Psalm while being hunted down by King Saul or when unjustly accused for his somewhat immodest dancing before God. Most of the time, it is only in the midst of being chased or unjustly accused that we recognize our deep need for God. But what strikes me in Psalm 131 is the posture of David, a posture of humility, recognition of his smallness, vulnerability, lack of capacity, and inability to save himself. The Psalmist doesn't even mention his accusers or his situation—we can only guess at that. Instead, his focus is on the God he has come to trust in such times as this.

Neither is David focused on a strategy to defend himself or even to escape the situation. Instead, he chooses to talk himself down from his perch of anxiety and fear by remembering God, a God portrayed as a mother in this Psalm. A mother who has weaned her child from the nourishment that the child had come to depend upon. David feels that absence of the nourishment for which he relied upon God in Psalm 23—this God who had before led him into green pastures and beside still waters now seems to have abandoned him. And yet he rests in God and God alone—no longer for what God can give or has given to him, but because God is his only rest and comfort. If he no longer receives anything else from God—if Michal's accusations stick or Saul catches up with David and takes his life, God is enough.

David has found a place of rest not in the good times but in the worst of times. To be unjustly accused and forced to run for our lives—and then to feel that what God has always given has been suddenly taken away—is a problematic place within which to experience rest. But David will have none of this. Our tendency is to fight our accusers or those who would destroy us and flee from God because he doesn't seem to care anymore. David responds as a child who, though not understanding their mother's actions, still trusts their mother and has learned to talk themselves back into the promises of God.

Last week, Heidi and I were staying with Ezra while his parents were at a meeting. We had a grand time playing together and then feeding Ezra his lunch. He was animated, laughed, shared new words, and was the life of our little party, seeming to relish that all of our focus and love was on him. But then it came time for his nap, and he suddenly became quite sober. He puckered his lips as if to cry and began repeating, "Mama, dada, nap, down, mama, dada, nap, mama, dada, nap, down," all the while looking as if he would at any moment break out into a loud sob. And we simply continued to console him that he was indeed correct—that after his nap, his mama and dada would be home, and he would be back downstairs with them. And when we laid him in his bed, he soon drifted off to sleep.

Heidi immediately observed that Ezra remarkably had been able to talk himself out of his anxiety and go to sleep peacefully.

And when Sarah and Jacob got home, Sarah shared that she had told Ezra that they would be home after his nap. Amid his fears and his absence from his parents, he was able to remind himself of their promise. He trusted them. Ezra believed his mom and dad. And this is what Psalm 131 is all about—remembering God because we have learned through our experience that God is trustworthy. We have learned, because of a life with God, that God keeps his promises. We have learned that God alone is enough for us because we have come to know God's love.

"Right now, dear God, today, at this moment, you know the battle and the injustice I face...I name it. Though I don't understand the whys or what the future holds, though it seems that everything I counted on, including you, is gone, I still and quiet my soul. Like a child who doesn't know where their parents went or why they are not with them, I remember—you promised you would never leave me or forsake me. After the darkness, after this nap, Mama, dada, mama, dada, mama, dada down. Amen."

CHAPTER 32

Ever Since That First Dismantling—We've Been Shaming and Blaming
April 18, 2021

The book of Genesis records that with the eating of the forbidden fruit, our first parents became self-aware in a way that they had not been before—they became aware that they had been dismantled and defrocked—and that their turning away from God had undone their innocence. Their response was to re-mantle themselves by hiding from their Creator, to cover up their newfound knowledge of their nakedness. But in God's mercy, God provided leather coverings for them.

The cost, however, was heavy to bear. Because in that one moment of turning from God, which was inevitably going to happen sometime to someone given the freedom that the Almighty had granted us, we began to blame one another for our shame and to shame ourselves for our blame.

But neither blame nor shame was ever God's intent for a people created in the divine image, and so the Trinity hatched a plan that included all three of them. The Father would send the Son to earth, and the Son would bring the Spirit with him. And in this way, the temporary covering of leather garments God had created for their nakedness would be replaced by a permanent healing of sin's pain, a permanent washing away of our blame, an endless undoing of the shame, and a permanent return to the Garden of Eden.

I will never forget the moment when my spiritual director, Eldon Fry, reminded me that "God never shames us." I will never forget it because, for some reason, quite truthfully, it was the first time that my spiritual ears had ever heard such good news. For I had lived as one who assumed that shame was from God, of God—and by God, I was going to live with it until one of those endless prayers for forgiveness finally pierced the heavenlies, and I would find peace. But until then, I would keep on counting up my sins and adding to my prayers for forgiveness hour by hour of just about every day. Yes, doing so failed to bring peace, but perhaps that was because my sin was so great. And so I would keep trying.

How long I had missed the good news that the loss of shame and blame were part of the Calvary deal—hatched in heaven by Father, Son, and Holy Spirit thousands of years before. It was on the cross that Christ took all of our shame and all of our blame so that St. Paul could rightfully declare that "there is no longer any condemnation for those who are in Christ Jesus!"

Jesus describes his mission as one of finally re-mantling us in Matthew 11, where he notes that he has mantled us with a new yoke, one that is now easy and with a burden that is light. The invitation is for the weary among us, wearing the mantle of shame and blame, to lay it down and to yoke up with Jesus. Simply by looking again at God's face seen in Christ himself.

Another interpretation of this passage is that the "yoke" was a mantle of identity that teachers or rabbis gave to their students to identify the rabbi to whom they belonged. "Come on," says our rabbi, "Take up my mantle and learn from me, for I am gentle and humble in heart, and you will find rest for your souls." While our turning from God had rendered us shame and blame and restlessness and wondering, our turning back to God would bring us a new identity as one of God's children and a new rest found only in this return.

Over this past year, the church as we've known it has been dismantled. It has both been taken apart, and its spiritual thinness and idolatry have been revealed. I was concerned as I began writing a year ago that we would try to re-mantle ourselves far too quickly, to put ourselves back together too soon to cover what had been exposed. I was concerned that we would not take time to allow God's Spirit to do the holy work required to re-mantle us. And I am more convinced than not that my worst fears have by and large come true. I believe that over this year, our anxieties and our efforts to re-mantle ourselves caused us to look in about every direction other than toward God.

I cling to the hope that God is not finished with any of us yet and that somewhere along the line, something was gained during this year—that we will slow down and allow our teacher to re-mantle us with his identity and with his yoke. As St. Augustine reminds us, we will be restless until we do so.

I also worry that we have gone further down the road of looking toward and embracing faces other than that of Christ, much as did the church of Germany in the 1930s. The result was that it was co-opted by the Third Reich, and it endorsed the deaths of millions. It did so by believing narratives, stories, and conspiracies that had no grounding in reality but promised to re-mantle a country devastated by World War I. And the promises of these narratives sounded too good to be true, and of course, they were.

While we are not Germany yet, similar seeds have been exposed that are present in much of today's evangelical church. And if we who are spiritual leaders in the church in this season do not confront them with the courage of Bonhoeffer and others now, we may witness these seeds bearing fruit sooner rather than later. And if that occurs, the dismantling that began this year will show itself to be only in its infancy.

CHAPTER 33

Oh My God! We've Been Dismantled and Forsaken!

April 17, 2021

Long before OMG was considered taking the Almighty's name in vain, it was a prayer—uttered no less than by the One who came to re-mantle us and to put his covering of wholeness and healing and compassion upon our broken and dismantled souls. And sometimes I wonder—when we the righteous are offended by those who use this refrain—OMG or "Oh my God"—whether the Almighty doesn't sometimes hear it also more like a prayer than as vain use of his identity. For it might be the closest thing to prayer that some folks ever get.

And I wonder, although I wasn't present, if it just wasn't the kind of prayer our first parents, discovering their nakedness, didn't utter as they looked embarrassingly at each others' bodies and cried out, "Oh my God, we've been dismantled. Our covering has been taken away, it has been removed from us, and we are now alone behind this tree."

But as always, even yet when we dismantle ourselves by turning our eyes from God, the Almighty came looking for and calling for the naked ones. "Where are you, my children? Why are you hiding from me?" "Well, because we're naked." And I suspect God just may have had a chuckle and thought, "Poor souls, you've been naked all along!" But instantaneously, Father, Son, and Spirit hatched a plan that would take thousands of years to reach fruition, but that would result in the re-mantling of those who chose to allow the covering of healing, wholeness, compassion, and love of the Crucified One to be placed upon them. How? By doing penance? No. By being good? No. By going to church then? No. By trying really hard? No. Simply, like the thief on the cross, turning our face back toward the loving and embracing and caring and receiving and compassionate face of Jesus.

There are many ways, said Martin Luther, to take the Almighty's name in vain. And words are only one of those ways. Every time we who claim to be followers of that name turn our faces to places and people and possessions other than Jesus—we have committed that same sin. And until we turn back—we will remain a dismantled bunch.

I've gotten some pretty strong resistance to the idea of a dismantled church and that God might be up to something so radical or destructive. But I'm not so sure anymore that it's God as much as we who are dismantling the church by taking our eyes off of Jesus and placing them elsewhere. Over the past year, the church had a chance in the midst of being dismantled, to gain traction with God, to be re-mantled by turning toward God's loving face from which the Psalmist says we can never, ever flee.

We turned instead to Donald Trump, to the safety of judges on the Supreme Court, to a march on Washington, D.C., in Jesus' name no less (talk about taking the Almighty's name in vain), and gave our attention and allegiance to the likes of Rush Limbaugh, theories ungrounded in reality, and claimed that being unmasked is our civil right. In the meantime, we called those who cared for the poor, who offered hope to those in the LGBTQ+ community, who opened their church doors as sanctuaries for immigrant children, who defended the brutality of police officers against African-American men who have been justifiably running from the police for three centuries—we called these the culturally compromised ones. Those who offered, like Jesus, a covering of wholeness and healing and forgiveness and grace and love—who offered the dismantled ones no less than a new divine mantle—were suddenly the compromised ones.

Friends, I'm not at all sure that Jesus sees it that way. I'm pretty sure he offers a new mantling to anyone who discovers that they are naked and dismantled, and in terror and fear, cries out, "Oh my God!"

PART SEVEN

A CHURCH
IN THE DARK

CHAPTER 34

The Dark Shadow of the Martyrs
January 13, 2021

In one of my podcast episodes last summer, I critiqued "the little church" down the street in my hometown for their sign that invited folks to a "call for prayer," nestled as it was between two huge red, white and blue wooden signs. I cautioned that such mixing of Christian faith and flag-waving was what sociologists have called "civil religion," but which the insurrection last week in our nation's capital reminds us is anything but civil. The mixing of Christian faith with political power always ends where such idolatry always ends— in flames, self-destruction, and the worshippers becoming what they worship.

The episode was entitled "100 Days of Prayer To the Red, White and Blue, the Compromised Church, and choosing Barabbas over Christ." When confronted last summer by a leader of this prayer gathering, I repented in the next episode. I described my strong reaction to the display of red, white, and blue banners surrounding an announcement for 100 days of prayer leading up to the U.S. Presidential election. I proceeded to point to this display as an example of what sociologists describe as civil religion. In any event, in repenting for the episode I said this:

> One of the values I learned from my father was that you should take care of it as soon as you can when you are wrong. I remember him calling folks up on the phone to take care of

129

wrongs he wanted to correct. A friend involved in the 100 days of prayer down the street rebuked my failure in misinterpreting their motives and for judging precisely what they were up to in that little church. He invited me to join them sometime.

I come from a theological tradition of Anabaptism that, from its early years, eschewed the sword and the power of the state and ran from the kind of religious synchronism that is represented by prayer meetings wrapped in Old Glory. I grew up in a home where we were taught NOT to pledge allegiance to the flag. And there is a good reason that in many churches with Anabaptist roots, the last thing you will find there is the American flag. I grieve that so many in my own tradition these days have been tempted by the power, status, and security that is promised but will never be fulfilled by any earthly government.

Our early notions as a nation that we were a beacon on a hill for the rest of the world, the whole idea of American exceptionalism, and the belief that God has given America a manifest destiny—all of these are powerful themes that get played out every day among evangelicals in the U.S. Ronald Reagan was particularly astute at wrapping American evangelicals in the same package as American triumphalism and patriotism. And Donald Trump has taken this slippery slope even further downhill by wrapping Christian faith up with American oppression and nationalism. What is so interesting to me is that of all the presidents since Jimmy Carter, these two (Reagan and Trump) have made less about even pretending to be Christian. Why in the world has the church allowed itself to be co-opted by the two presidents who apparently cared so little about cultivating a personal life with God?

The problem for the church is that American civil religion boils God down to a generic deity that stands in for whatever happens to be, well, red, white, and blue. If it is going to make America great again, then it must be what God wants. Intriguingly, the very evangelicals who are so offended when they can't use the name of Jesus in the public square are the same ones who have fallen for the empty, powerless, useless, and nameless god of American civil religion.

In the Old Testament, God warned Samuel that this is where his people would end up if they chose a king rather than the King. They would end up as they did on the day of our Lord's crucifixion, choosing Barabbas over the One dying up there on that tree—that one who looks so powerless, so unexceptional, so untriumphant, so unpatriotic. Even Barabbas looked more kingly than Christ. Get him off of there they cried to Pilate; we have to worship God tomorrow. And we need to get our flags ready also.

Perhaps repenting for my attitude was appropriate. But my critique was right on. For it turns out that one of the leaders of that prayer gathering helped organize four busloads from my hometown to take that trip to Washington, D.C., last week and participate in the march on the Capitol. Sometimes, friends, those of us steeped in the shadow of the martyrs need to pay greater attention to our instincts. Those instincts might just be the voice of our Lord reminding us in the Gospel of Luke, chapter 9:

> Then he said to them all, "If any want to become my followers, let them deny themselves and take up their cross daily and follow me. For those who want to save their life will lose it, and those who lose their life for my sake will save it. What does it profit them if they gain the whole world, but lose or forfeit themselves? Those who are ashamed of me and of my words, of them the Son of Man will be ashamed when he comes in his glory and the glory of the Father and of the holy angels." (Luke 9:23-26)

My backtracking this summer from my comments was perhaps a lesson in cowardice rather than a profile in courage. I've taken many hits over the years for the willingness I've had to raise questions and challenge taken for granted realities of those in the church. And again, perhaps it was above all, my heart that needed to be more like Christ's. If last week illustrates anything, it should remind us of Jesus' words that "those who live by the sword will die by the sword," as will so many of those who join the mobs. And it won't matter whether their t-shirts or flags say, "Jesus saves." But I do know one thing, Christ would not have participated in that march on Washington, D.C., and anyone who believes otherwise has fallen far from the gospel and the freedom that is found in laying down one's life rather than taking up one's sword.

Those who carry those flags and wear those t-shirts seem to have forgotten that what Jesus saves is not democracy or religious freedom. Neither of these is promoted or endorsed in Scripture. What Jesus saves us from is the kind of death that we saw so clearly perpetrated in images I will never forget. He keeps us from the need to defend ourselves. He saves us from the compulsion to protect our interests.

When we get to that point, my friends, there is no stopping the coming Kingdom—pure and undefiled by political power and corruption. He calls us to stand with him, to carry that cross that was carried by our martyr ancestors, that cross that speaks of God's reign and God's order and God's kingdom, and a cross that promises my enemy who threatens me and destroys me—that I will not return the favor. I am free from revenge. I am free to love. And I am free to be courageous.

As I have said repeatedly to our congregation and did so again this past Sunday, this year's election will be nothing more than a footnote in God's story of his Kingdom and Reign. So where do you want to end up, friend—in the footnotes or the center of the Story? Today, I'm thankful for the shadow of the martyrs in my church history, even though theirs was a high bar for me as a kid to imagine reaching. But given Jesus' words, reaching that bar is less about doing than about giving up, surrendering our lives to him, and in the process, finding that one day we will be among those who get our lives back. What a glorious day that will be!

The question, "Would you die for Jesus?" tormented me as a child, struggling as I was with the terror of a God who would send me into hellfire if I said, "No" or "I'm not sure." Thinking of that question last week in light of the events in Washington, D.C.— brought great peace and a sense of freedom to realize that, by this point in my life, the answer to that question just might be, "I think so."

CHAPTER 35

A Church Traumatized and Dismantled—Then and Now

January 7, 2021

When God's people were exiled into Babylon in the 6th century B.C., the experience they had we would commonly today identify as culture shock and trauma. They had been stripped of all that they knew to be real and true in the world. The temple was dismantled. Yahweh had all but abandoned them. And the lies they had believed had all turned out to be just lies. Their culture (beliefs, values, norms) was in shreds. Their typical rituals and forms of social interaction were gone, and any structure or organization that gave them guardrails and landmarks to guide them.

Quite likely, they were experiencing what sociologists call anomie—that sense of nothingness, of standing on the edge of an abyss and looking down into blackness. Anomie is fed by the upending of all that we know to be normal and predictable and dependable, as well as by social isolation.

Friends, we are a society that about as clearly reflects these anomic qualities as any most of us have experienced, aside from our brothers and sisters of color and far too many women who have been victims of trauma and abuse. But for those in the center of society, this is a cliff we have never stood at the edge of before.

But this is where God's people were in Jeremiah's day. And then they get a letter from the prophet—the only prophet among them who had accurately predicted that this day of judgment would come. I suspect the letter was opened with a good deal of expectation that Jeremiah would now rub salt in the wounds of those who so long had decried his words.

But instead, Jeremiah opens with this:

> This is what the Lord Almighty, the God of Israel, says to all those I carried into exile from Jerusalem to Babylon: "Build houses and settle down; plant gardens and eat what they produce. Marry and have sons and daughters; find wives for your sons and give your daughters in marriage so that they too may have sons and daughters. Increase in number there; do not decrease. Also, seek the peace and prosperity of the city to which I have carried you into exile. Pray to the Lord for it because if it prospers, you too will prosper." Yes, this is what the Lord Almighty, the God of Israel, says: "Do not let the prophets and diviners among you deceive you. Do not listen to the dreams you encourage them to have. They are prophesying lies to you in my name. I have not sent them," declares the Lord. (Jeremiah 29:4-9, NIV)

Unbelievable, what was Yahweh doing now? Well, through Jeremiah, God was resetting the culture, structure, and rituals that had been lost in the transition to Babylon. What people paralyzed by culture shock needed to hear was not, "I told you so," or more judgment, shame, and condemnation. What they needed to hear were words reminding them of who they were and whose they were. That before they had so failed to be a people of shalom, they had been a people of shalom. That before they had abandoned Yahweh for other gods, they had been the people of Yahweh. That before they had done such injustice to the marginalized, they had been people who cared for the poor and widows and orphans. And the key to becoming these people again would be, well, beginning to become this kind of people again. Recover the culture. Rebuild the structures. And by the way, throw a party for your kids when they get married. And lastly, don't stop reproducing the blessings of childhood and the reminder of all reminders that life and goodness continue in the midst of death and evil. And by the way, God says, I still have plans "to prosper you." I still have "plans to give you a hope and a future." In other words, they could be even among their enemies, the people of God's reign, of God's order, who proclaimed God's peace and prosperity to their worst enemies. God says the way to experience my shalom is to offer it to the world around you—then it will come back to you!

This morning, you and I awakened to a land that has been shattered by an unbelievable attack on the U.S. Capitol building, to a reality that has become disorienting, and to violent images that, for the rest of our lives, we will never forget. What we thought was true no longer is, and we now see what we thought was real was not. And sadly, those among us who have experienced the most trauma in our lives and communities are now the ones most deeply re-traumatized by the events of last week and this year.

But it is precisely because they have known trauma that we must now listen to their voices, and God forgive us for not doing so sooner. It is the women in our Christian communities who have known trauma but have too long been sidelined, and we must look to them now to remind us of how one finds hope, how one rebuilds, and how one moves forward in a dismantled and traumatized church to offer shalom to a broken world. It is to our brothers and sisters of color, who have long found ways to declare hope and life and amid oppression, who know how to build and dance and sing in the face of evil, and who have long offered shalom (though shalom was the last thing anyone was offering them) that we must now turn for guidance and help and direction.

For the rational, clean, predictable, professional world built by those in the center, those with power, mainly those of us who are white males, is tottering, leaning, and unlikely to lead us toward the new heaven and the new earth. For a good reason, our Lord promised that "the first will be last and the last will be first."

CHAPTER 36

God Is Dead, and the Downside of This Side of the Resurrection
April 3, 2021

This is Holy Saturday, made holy not because the news is good but indeed the opposite—the worst news possible. God is dead. There is no promise for tomorrow. The enemy has won. We were so close to winning the war, so close to seeing all of creation come to life in a cacophony of awakening sounds from graves, hospitals, morgues, addiction treatment facilities, prisons, half-way houses, shelters for victims of domestic violence, streets where those of color are forced to the ground crying out for life like their ancestors centuries before, those cast aside from a church that offered no hope because they couldn't keep the rules, and from the self-righteous within that church that also broke the rules but had crafted covers for their sins. We had expected the light to break through from all of these quarters, new songs to emerge, the promise of a new future, justice to reign, and evil to be overcome.

For that had been the assurance, the guarantee of this One who had begun his ministry by declaring that he would do precisely these things—free captives, set prisoners free, make the blind see, and finally, bring in the justice of the year of Jubilee.

But today, we recognize that it was all such a hoax. Like so many pretenders before him, except that he was better at his magic tricks than most of them, he turned out to just be one more snake oil salesman.

But he certainly did seem to believe in his product. He stuck to his story to the bitter end even if his followers didn't. He even seemed to have half a hunch that his death was just part of the deal and that he just might return from his little visit into the depths of hell itself, where like the Energizer Bunny, he just kept setting people free. So on this day between days, this day between promise lost and whatever lies ahead, perhaps it is best not to lose all hope, not to cash in our chips too early, not to leave that cross just yet. Because who knows, maybe the One who said all things are possible just might have one more trick up his sleeve, or maybe not.

I don't know what it was like to follow this prophet and mystic from Galilee on Holy Saturday. But I do know, as do you, that we can identify if we are honest, with what it must have felt like to have seen one's hopes and dreams go down with the Messiah's death on Good Friday. Because again, if we are honest, many of our hopes and dreams still seem to go so unfulfilled.

This is why I am troubled by those who gloss over Holy Saturday, who so quickly want to move us to Easter Sunday. You know, the preachers who yell at the top of their lungs, "Friday is here, but Sunday's-comin'!" I know. Most of them mean well. They intend to give us hope. The problem is that for many of us, and those around us, the despair of Saturday, the darkness of Saturday, the fear of Saturday, the shame felt on Saturday, the abandonment of Saturday keeps us from really being able to hear or believe the promise of Sunday.

I am thankful that the prophet and mystic from Nazareth experienced Saturday and that the Father allowed him to do so. And somehow, from what the Scripture suggests about his being able to feel our pain yet today, I can't help but believe and be grateful that though he experienced Sunday's life, he carries with him still a bit of Saturday's death. And for this reason, is still able to bear our sorrows, take our pain, and walk with us through the valley of the shadow of death.

CHAPTER 37

Doing Church "Right" and Escaping the World
April 8, 2021

I am growing in my concerns about the church as we have socially constructed it these days, for increasingly, it just doesn't sound like the church Jesus intended. I recently read the description of a weekend event being proposed by a church that sounded like the kind of language one might expect from a church of the 1950s perhaps—hunkering down, closing the hatches, fortifying itself against a dangerous world.

Too often, we have erroneously called for the church to be separated from the world, even though Jesus prayed that we would not be taken out of the world but protected from the enemy. Because as our Lord himself knew, Satan was as likely to show up at the Last Supper as he was in the desert, and perhaps is more dangerous at the Last Supper than even in the desert where we might expect to find the foe of our souls.

As I've noted before, as a kid in Sunday school, I had a visceral reaction to my teacher, who taught us that the world was a dangerous and evil place. No, I thought, the devil is in this church as much as in that world. And these days, perhaps four or five decades later, I believe that even more. The more I hear from listeners, the more convinced I am that it may be within the church rather than the world that the most significant harm has been done to the gospel and to the little ones who in our neglect and abuse have abandoned the church—not because the world is so attractive but merely because it feels safer.

I grieve a lot these days. I mourn the ignorance of a church that has abandoned our Black brothers and sisters and believes systemic racism is a political stunt or the latest fad. I grieve a church where men are given free rein to harm the vulnerable. I grieve a church where since Covid-19, we have become more myopic and self-focused, revealed in how we spent the last year debating masks and marching on the Capitol rather than deepening our life with God. When I asked someone whom I trust why the church has retrenched and hunkered down, his response was immediate, "because evangelicals lost the Presidential election." A local leader likes to call the progressive churches in our community the "compromised churches." And yet, it was the "uncompromised" churches in our town that chartered four buses to attend the rally that turned into an insurrection on January 6.

I grieve a church that takes upon itself the task of separating the goats from the sheep by calling out compromised versus uncompromised. I'm afraid some of us will be very surprised when the Matthew 25 reckoning occurs—for indeed, there was lots of surprise going around that day. And there's nigh a word about defending our rights or protecting our favored position because those on the left were too busy doing real Kingdom work to care about what they gained or lost:

> When the Son of Man comes in his glory, and all the angels with him, then he will sit on the throne of his glory. All the nations will be gathered before him, and he will separate people from one another as a shepherd separates the sheep from the goats, and he will put the sheep at his right hand and the goats

at the left. Then the king will say to those at his right hand, "Come, you that are blessed by my Father, inherit the kingdom prepared for you from the foundation of the world; for I was hungry and you gave me food, I was thirsty and you gave me something to drink, I was a stranger and you welcomed me, I was naked and you gave me clothing, I was sick and you took care of me, I was in prison and you visited me." Then the righteous will answer him, "Lord, when was it that we saw you hungry and gave you food, or thirsty and gave you something to drink? And when was it that we saw you a stranger and welcomed you, or naked and gave you clothing? And when was it that we saw you sick or in prison and visited you?" And the king will answer them, "Truly I tell you, just as you did it to one of the least of these who are members of my family, you did it to me." Then he will say to those at his left hand, "You that are accursed, depart from me into the eternal fire prepared for the devil and his angels; for I was hungry and you gave me no food, I was thirsty and you gave me nothing to drink, I was a stranger and you did not welcome me, naked and you did not give me clothing, sick and in prison and you did not visit me." Then they also will answer, "Lord, when was it that we saw you hungry or thirsty or a stranger or naked or sick or in prison, and did not take care of you?" Then he will answer them, "Truly I tell you, just as you did not do it to one of the least of these, you did not do it to me." And these will go away into eternal punishment, but the righteous into eternal life. (Matthew 25: 31-46)

CHAPTER 38

Why the Mountains Must Be Removed so the Diaspora Can Come Home
May 7, 2021

In his little book *Freeway Under Construction by Order of Isaiah 40:3-5*, by charismatic preacher Judson Cornwall that captured my attention as a kid, Cornwall laments that there is no multi-lane highway to God but only little-used antiquated byways. But he says:

> Still men [and women] have an inner yearning after God...when this hunger grips the world, as the prophets have declared it would, there must be a rapid, safe, enjoyable access to God. The rituals, the catechisms, religious activities, and trappings will not appeal to this group of people. They will need a multi-lane freeway into God's presence, and the time to build it is before it is so desperately needed.[34]

What I have been writing over the past year has been most received by those who are restless with the church's current status and have either left the church or feel marginalized in it. For some, leaving was perhaps the only safe alternative. As a pastor couple for the past ten years, Heidi and I have insisted that our congregation be a safe and nurturing space for children and others who are most vulnerable to abuse and violation by those with power. We have also learned that taking such a stand is costly and one had better be pre-

---

[34] *Freeway Under Construction.*

pared to stand alone some days. I have repeatedly said that racism in the church and our society might not be dismantled until the church itself is dismantled. And I also wonder now about the abuse and violation of the most vulnerable that has far too often occurred within the context of the church. Is it possible that God's dismantling of the church has anything at all to do with the church's failure to dismantle abuse by priests, pastors, and other leaders? Are we facing the repercussions of our failures to protect those whom Christ came to both save and protect?

I recently heard this from a student about her experience in the church:

> I never grew up in a religious setting. My parents wanted me to form my own ideas about the world, so they never made us go to church. When I was in 8th grade, my one Christian friend, who is still involved with the church, invited me to go to her youth group and I continued to go until senior year. I learned valuable lessons that really helped me in high school and became really close with my friends. But I really didn't understand the whole God thing, which really frustrated me because everyone who I had surrounded myself with did. So, I really tried to put in some extra effort and understand it, but I just couldn't. I don't know how people can just blindly follow something that just seems fictitious. The nail in the coffin for me and the thing that really pulled me away from joining anything religious again was honestly the people in the religion and how they think their way of thinking is the only correct way. For example, when it became election year and I could vote, I became obsessed about learning everything/anything relating to politics. I spent countless hours digging through research, polls, studies, articles, etc. trying to understand the most debated about topics and trying to form a justified, fair

opinion about what I had learned. I tried to look at every side or every opinion a person could have just to get a well-rounded perspective. But when it came time for me to look into abortion, I really couldn't avoid the onslaught of religious based, pro-lifers projecting their own beliefs onto me. Not to mention, the immense amount of false information and fear they spread to countless other women to prevent them from aborting a baby they simply can't take care of. This continual pattern of Christians/Catholics/etc... portraying their ideas, on certain topics (like abortion or even Covid-19), as the **only** correct way of thinking just made me really frustrated. Anyways, all of this to say, I do not like having other people's personal ideas and beliefs being forced upon me. Essentially, I am not religious because I cannot blindly follow something I don't understand or believe, and I do not like how ideologically suppressive religions tend to be. Again, I am not saying all churches, religions, and people are like this, but I experienced this.

It is easy for we who are in the church to ignore those leaving the church in droves these days, and to point to their failures to assimilate to the church culture, their differences of agreement with our theology and practice, their pain and woundedness that kept them from forgiving and on and on. The problem is that these are precisely the people that drew themselves to Jesus and to whom Jesus was drawn. There was a reason that wounded women so loved this man and that he loved them. While sociologists call such folks religious "nones" these days, I think of them as the diaspora whom Jesus is searching for, the sheep who he said are not yet in his fold, the children of God with his imprint upon them even if they don't know it. What would it take for the church to become a place for the questions of my student to be engaged with grace, the wounds of sexual survivors to be cared for and healed, and the diaspora to be welcomed back home?

In this increasingly post-COVID world, it is easy for us, having experienced a bit of dismantling of our churchly mountains, to try to get back to life, as usual, hoping that the worst is behind us. But Judson Cornwall warns us:

> How quickly we Christians compensate for the losses the Spirit has extracted from our lives. We rationalize that if He didn't allow trees, he would be satisfied with grass and wildflowers. Anything we can produce seems superior to the barrenness of the moment...Obviously we still haven't understood God's purpose in building a freeway through our life. We're still trying to assist Him...not realizing that all of our help is but a hindrance.

If the church becomes a place for doubters, the wounded, and the diaspora, I think the Spirit's got a bit more excavation and dismantling to do of our high places in the church. So hold on for the ride, folks—this ain't going to be like anything we've seen in our lifetime!

CHAPTER 39

Hunkering Down, Hellfire, and Culture Wars—How About Grace?

April 21, 2021

O ver the past century, as the impact of modernity with its accompanying rationality, secularization, geographic mobility, higher levels of education, and affluence began to have its affect upon evangelicals, including Anabaptist followers of Jesus, it seems to me that we have often tried just about every alternative except Jesus. As Mennonites in the front end of the 20th century, we reinforced the need to hunker down—at least in my neck of the woods. We would become even more plain, even more committed to separation from that evil and dangerous world. We would double down on the teaching that godliness, as we understood it, was measured by our distance from the world that God so loved and so loves still.

Early Anabaptist leader Michael Sattler had stated that "Christ despises the world; His children shall do the same." The problem is that it is terribly difficult to carry out the last words of Jesus about bringing the good news to a broken world when we've barricaded ourselves against that world. The only thing to do is to lob tracts about four spiritual laws across lawns and toward front doors and hope that in reading about these laws, our neighbors become as bound up about their holiness as we are.

Unfortunately, hunkering down only works when your culture contains the carrot of strong community and the stick of shunning and ex-communication. Modernity guaranteed that few of us—except for some subcultural and counter-cultural groups—would be able to enjoy eating carrots while simultaneously using those carrots as sticks to beat over the head those who decided that the carrots were rotten. A bit strong? Depends on whether the carrots taste sweet to you or not. But hunkering down was not going to work with evangelical youth who had tasted the allure of other carrots and within communities that increasingly had fewer sticks to yield.

So the church tried revival meetings—sending out mercenaries like George Brunk II to beat those who had backslidden into submission by holding hell over our heads. Yesterday, one listener reported being in one of those tent meetings in the middle of a storm while George urged the choir to keep singing because his tent had never blown down before. Moments later, perhaps as a word about the coming dismantling of the church, the canvas contraption fell over. "Scared the hell out of us," this listener said.

One of the many problems with this revival approach was that while beating the hell out of us, it was never clear what we would replace that hell with. It reminds me of Jesus' words that you can exorcise the demon, but it returns with seven friends unless it is replaced. And for me, with my obsessive-compulsive struggle and religious preoccupation with my certain damnation, the demons kept returning. And one more sinner's prayer never seemed to make a difference. For it wasn't the eradication of sin I needed; it was a word that I was deeply loved and accepted by a caring Creator who watches even the sparrow fall and knew how many hairs I had on my head, even as one more prayer warrior thanked God for this child who had finally given his life to Jesus. The problem was, it was not my first time to the altar by a long shot, and I was still in the dark about God's grace.

It would be as a first-year student at Wheaton College that I discovered a different message—the one that my Pap had been quietly singing all the while I heard the more dominant tune of hell-fire and brimstone. For all of his problems, I found to my great relief a kindred spirit in Martin Luther. Luther too, had found that the church offered only bondage and who, perhaps with his version of obsessive-compulsive disorder, discovered that the "just shall live by faith" and that "it is by grace that one is saved." I will never forget the relief I felt, the comfort I found, and the hope I discovered. These things would be temporary balms for a soul that had such a deficit as mine, but this was the beginning, and I would come back to Luther's *Freedom of a Christian* year after year as my soul needed reminding.[35] Again, like hunkering down against the world had failed to save us and retain our children, so instilling in us that we were innately evil would serve to keep many of us in therapy for a lifetime.

Finally, and again while I was at Wheaton College, the church would try the third alternative. If hunkering down against the world and threatening our kids with hellfire had not kept them from joining the hippies, wearing mini-skirts, and experimenting with pot hadn't worked, well then in God's name, we would militarize against the culture by joining the political right. And so the likes of Jerry Falwell, Bob Jones, Pat Robertson, and a host of others would combine forces with Ronald Reagan and show the liberal and godless left-wing that the evangelical right-wing had the corner on morality. Suddenly a church and political party that had shown little concern about Rowe v. Wade at the time when the Supreme Court came down on the side of abortion (which, by the way, I am finding my students increasingly opposing less for religious reasons alone but because science and technology are showing us a little child in there

---

35   Martin Luther, *Freedom of a Christian* (Muhlenberg Press, 1957).

after all), found a new cause and would use it to wield their power against the godless culture within which their kids were increasingly at home.

But folks, it is abundantly clear that the church sold its soul to the devil. For forty years, the church has compromised its moral clarity, abandoned the Jesus of the Gospels, and forsaken its future by counting on the security of Supreme Court justices and the empty promises of presidents without moral compasses.

But still, our youth are leaving us. And why not? We've offered them every alternative in the book except the One about whom the Book is about after all. The died and resurrected One who came not to keep us out of the world but to pray for our protection from the evil one, whose only words of hellfire and brimstone were for the self-righteous rather than those who knew better than any that they were lost, and who on his way to the cross that was its own kind of insurrection ordered his disciples to put away their swords since "those who live by the sword will die by the sword."

As I face a classroom full of students who are in deep pain, who jokingly but not really, respond to "How are you doing" with "I'm dead," who more than ever struggle with anxiety and depression, and who claim gender identities not recognized in the church—I will not separate myself from them, I will not preach hellfire and brimstone, and I will not militarize against them or their culture. No, I will stay with my students who so much need the good news that over the past year I finally found. And if it took a pastor that many decades, why shouldn't I be patient with them. For if it's not good news for them it's also not good news for me either.